"Tracie Braylock offers protective care ~~~ book *Radical Relaxation*, she undergirds professional knowledge, spiritual practices, and self-care with God's Word and transformative prayers. She graciously invites the reader into a guided tour that is designed to release stress through healing, rest, and relaxation. She comprehensively guides the participant to intentional Selah moments."

Barbara L. Peacock, founder of Peacock Soul Care and author of *Soul Care in African American Practice*

"Wow! I didn't realize how much I needed this book! Tracie Braylock writes like a somatic prophet urging us to return to our Creator and care for the good bodies we have been given. Her breadth of experience and depth of faith helped me connect the dots between God's Word and the blessed relaxation that awaits us. If stress is your enemy, get this book and heed her call to reorientation, rootedness, rest, and a reimagined life with God."

Jason Cusick, lead pastor at Journey of Faith in Southern California and author of *The Anxiety Field Guide*

"I didn't know how much I would need this book during the midlife season I am walking through, but *Radical Relaxation* is my new field guide to unknown healing and a deeper level of embodied relaxation. Tracie Braylock gently empowers her readers to take control of their bodies, minds, and souls. Throughout these pages, you'll appreciate Tracie's medical expertise as she seamlessly integrates real-life guidance with relevant Scripture passages. Thanks to Tracie, I now feel fully equipped to trust the body God has gifted me as I find realignment and renewal more holistically."

Jodi H. Grubbs, author of *Live Slowly*

"From one friend to another, Tracie Braylock speaks from the heart, urging us toward change. Integrating her experience as a surgical nurse, Braylock weaves together medical metaphors with engaging stories from the hospital, equipping us with practical and holistic wisdom about the importance of addressing stress in our bodies. Taking concrete steps towards well-being is not an option but a necessity. Thanks for this labor of love!"

Bethany Dearborn Hiser, spiritual director and author of *From Burned Out to Beloved: Soul Care for Wounded Healers*

radical relaxation

Releasing the Stress You Were Never Meant to Carry

TRACIE BRAYLOCK

An imprint of InterVarsity Press
Downers Grove, Illinois

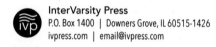

InterVarsity Press
P.O. Box 1400 | Downers Grove, IL 60515-1426
ivpress.com | email@ivpress.com

InterVarsity Press® is the publishing division of InterVarsity Christian Fellowship/USA®. For more information, visit intervarsity.org.

All Scripture quotations, unless otherwise indicated, are taken from The Holy Bible, New International Version®, NIV®. Copyright © 1973, 1978, 1984, 2011 by Biblica, Inc.™ Used by permission of Zondervan. All rights reserved worldwide. www.zondervan.com. The "NIV" and "New International Version" are trademarks registered in the United States Patent and Trademark Office by Biblica, Inc.™

While any stories in this book are true, some names and identifying information may have been changed to protect the privacy of individuals.

The publisher cannot verify the accuracy or functionality of website URLs used in this book beyond the date of publication.

Cover design: Faceout Studio
Interior design: Jeanna Wiggins
Cover images: Shutterstock, 1937151346 and 1897654075
Interior image: 692621800, zzayko, iStock / Getty Images Plus

ISBN 978-1-5140-0944-4 (print) | ISBN 978-1-5140-0945-1 (digital)

Printed in the United States of America ♾

Library of Congress Cataloging-in-Publication Data
A catalog record for this book is available from the Library of Congress.

32   31   30   29   28   27   26   25 | 13   12   11   10   9   8   7   6   5   4   3   2   1

To my children,

Richmond, Solomon, Bria, and Zara

Thank you for filling my life with wonder.

I'm continuously in awe of each of you.

May you always know how deeply loved you are and

remember that nothing is impossible with God.

Continue to be the salt and light you're created to be.

I love you.

Contents

Introduction

HEY, FRIEND. YOU MAY BE WONDERING if this book is worth your time. So I'm going to tell you why I wrote it and why I believe it's important for you to read.

I used to work in the operating room, where stress abounds. From the patient in need of the operation, to the surgeon trusted and tasked with performing the surgical procedure, to the team who works tirelessly to ensure the best possible outcome for the patient.

But stress isn't confined to the walls of the operating room. It's everywhere, and there's virtually nothing left uncontaminated by it.

Stress fuels our sleepless nights and exhausted days. It goes to work with us and is waiting with open arms on our commutes and in our homes. Stress infiltrates our relationships, with God, ourselves, and others. And it doesn't care at all about our hopes, dreams, aspirations, or mission. Stress seeks to kill, steal, and destroy, separating us from the truth, distracting us from the present, and making the peace available to us seem out of reach.

So how do you stop stress in a world filled with chaos and dis-ease, a world that has become dismissive about how you're created and seems to champion the very stress you war against each day?

You start by reminding yourself that you are not of the world, nor do you belong to it, and you redirect your attention to the truth that there's another way of being in this world. A better, divinely knit-together way of existing that amplifies your power, your potential, and God's promises for your life. Then you get radical!

In health care, to have a radical procedure means to remove the disease, its root, and all of the surrounding tissue that's diseased or potentially diseased. This application of *radical* means you're severing stress, the roots of your stress, and everything surrounding you that's causing you stress.

This isn't a form of punishment, nor is it meant to make you destroy relationships or hastily quit your job. This involves a thorough, strategically mapped-out plan to ensure your healing and longevity, with the intention of cutting off stress and its harmful effects so that you can be present to carry out your divine assignments in this world.

My friend, this book isn't filled with quick fixes for your stress. It's a guide toward lifelong transformation. A body of work designed to encourage and support you, while challenging you to expand your way of thinking, living, and being.

This book is an invitation to reorient to how you're designed, become rooted in healing, rest in your radical nature, and reimagine your future with less stress and more relaxation. And I'm guiding you every step of the way.

1

Wonderfully Made

THERE I AM, STANDING ON A PLATFORM, peering over the blue surgical drapes into the body of a patient having open-heart surgery. While watching the heartbeat and blood pulse through the vessels within this cavity, I didn't consider the various life circumstances that led this person to the operating room table, the trauma and pain endured, or the stressors that weighed heavily upon them throughout their lives. I simply loved witnessing the intricacies that comprise the human body. Each organ, vessel, and body system divinely positioned to make one's existence possible. With every pulse, breath, and nerve signal comes a new possibility, a chance to co-create with God and leave your fingerprints on eternity.

Taking what was formless and void, God created the heavens and the earth, the wonders of which have been studied for millennia and still are not fully understood. With the same divine imagination, he formed the human body and called it good, creating systems that can function with, and without, your participation, and processes that enable healing to occur whether or not you are aware of your own wounds. God breathed into you the breath of life while weaving wisdom into every cell. You are indeed fearfully and wonderfully made, and it's vital that you learn how.

Whether you find yourself in awe of how your body works, or if discussions about the human body make you feel a bit awkward, I'm here to help you take a deeper look into your masterful design. I'm here to remind you that before you were formed in your mother's womb, God knew you. You are so valuable that God has numbered the very hairs on your head. Your body, including every curve and challenge it may carry, is considered God's temple, and the Holy Spirit dwells within you. Therefore, it's critical that you learn what your body is capable of. Acknowledging your body's delicacy and divinity, as a museum curator appreciates works of art. Tending to and preserving it with care and dedication. Adopting healing practices and identifying the underutilized gems woven into your physical being as if your life were on exhibit. A reflection of your Creator, a faithful steward and safe handler of the precious gifts within you. A soul wrapped in the form the Potter's hands deemed good for you to journey in. Skin, bones, muscles, and nerve fibers working in collaboration to produce life within and through you. You, my friend, are holy.

YOU ARE THE LIGHT

A patient was having a laparoscopy, the type of operation that gives the surgeon access to the abdomen or pelvis through small incisions in the skin while using the aid of a camera.

Once the camera is inside the body cavity, images of the interior of the abdomen or pelvis are relayed to a monitor. As an operating room nurse, my role in this particular operation was to hold the camera. The camera holder is required to have a steady hand and must remain attentive to the operation, guiding the camera as directed so the surgeon can see the area of the body they're working on.

Every now and then, the laparoscopic camera can touch something inside the body cavity, obscuring the lens and obstructing the view. When this happens, the camera must be removed from the body and cleaned off so that the light and internal structures are visible again.

No matter how steady my hand, how skilled the surgeon, or how safe the procedure typically is, without the light source that shines through the scope, the operation could not take place. The light is necessary because the space where the work takes place is dark and, in many cases, has never been exposed to light. Without the light, the operation, healing, and restoration wouldn't happen.

When you seem to keep bumping into one stressor after another in your life, you have to take some time to remove it and clean yourself off from its effects. If you don't, the stress can obstruct your view, resulting in the dimming of your light, and may even cause you to forget your own worth and wonder. Although your light is still present, stress can act as a distraction, leaving you discouraged or experiencing feelings of defeat. So let this be your reminder: You are the light of the world, designed to shine into the darkness and illuminate the lives of people and spaces, including some that have yet to be exposed to the light. Your light enables others to see your good deeds and glorify God in heaven, so don't allow stress to stop you from shining and sharing who you are.

INNATE HEALING WISDOM

The human body has the capacity to heal itself, working on your behalf, often beyond your conscious awareness. Your body constantly adapts for you, seeking a state of balance among all of your body systems, called homeostasis, which is necessary for your survival and the proper function of the body.

Whether you're undergoing a surgical procedure or you cut yourself in your kitchen, as soon as you are wounded, your body takes action. Your platelets begin to clot and the blood vessels that have been cut begin to constrict. This phase, called hemostasis, keeps you from losing too much blood.

Your mast cells also release substances filled with enzymes and histamine that cause inflammation and the characteristic signs of redness, heat, swelling, and pain around the wound site. Your white blood cells move into the wound, acting as infection control agents dispatched to fight off bacteria and clean the wound of debris. These are functions of the inflammatory phase.

Next is the proliferative phase, when the rebuilding process begins. Your cells start to multiply and spread. New cells start filling in the wound, forming new tissue known as granulation tissue. Your body forms new blood vessels to deliver a sufficient amount of oxygen and nutrients to the new tissue. Your wound edges are pulled together as the new granulation tissue forms. Your wound is then layered with epithelial cells, the type of cells that cover the surface of your body.

Your wound then enters the maturation, or remodeling, phase. Your wound achieves maximum strength and flexibility at this stage. Cells that are no longer needed in the healing process are removed, reducing the thickness of the scar, and a process called cross-linking occurs in which collagen fibers align to thin and strengthen the skin.

This very intricate and complex cascade and overlapping sequence of events displays the human body's resilience. Your body is innately designed to fight for you and built to bounce back when faced with challenges and stressors that disrupt its normal equilibrium. You see, your body has been divinely programmed to keep you alive, so it doesn't wait for your permission, and in many cases, it doesn't even require your participation before responding.

And still, in the midst of this deeply rooted wisdom, you can influence and improve your physical resilience and the speed at which you cycle through the healing process. Because the efficiency of your healing and your body's sense of harmony are heavily impacted by your ability to remain well nourished, rested, and relaxed.

WHO GOD SAYS YOU ARE

Every patient who requires hospital care is given a new ID wristband containing all of the information about who they are and who's in charge of their care. This ID efficiently communicates sensitive data to hospital personnel within a demanding health care environment so that each patient is correctly identified and able to receive their customized care. Becoming a believer in Christ also gives you a new ID that communicates your identity to the world. Your ID says that you are created in the image of God and your identity is solely found in him. If you've ever struggled to remember that I want to remind you of who God says you are.

Your God-given identity. Years ago, hospital personnel identified patients by their illnesses—the kidney stones in 405 or the heart murmur in 211. Not only did this practice lack compassion, it dehumanized the individual, dismissing and devaluing their wholeness, blinding caregivers to deeper levels of empathy, and trivializing an autonomous person down to a problem to be solved.

Describing someone by the type of illness they're experiencing doesn't take valuable characteristics into account, such as their age and overall health status, and often leads to errors in patient identification.

Patient misidentification has repeatedly led to medication, testing, and transfusion errors. It's caused patients to receive the wrong procedure and infants to be discharged to the wrong family.

The misidentification of patients, and the well-documented history of errors that have resulted because of it, caused the identification process to undergo a shift. Health care workers now involve the patient in the process and use two patient identifiers, such as one's name and date of birth, when identifying their patients. This greatly improves the reliability that the correct patient will receive the correct treatment or service.

Misidentification can also take place in your life. It occurs when you begin to conform to the patterns of this world, or when you're confused about who you are because of the stories that you have heard from yourself and from others.

So if we were together right now, I'd look into your eyes and ask, "How are you identifying yourself? Are the narratives and names you're applying to yourself true?" Because, my friend, any misidentification taking place in your life is contributing to your stress and your ongoing wounding. It's causing preventable errors in judgment and keeping you in cycles of stress that could be healed if you properly identify and treat them.

If you recognize that you have misidentified yourself in one way or another, there are two spiritual identifiers that can help bring you back into alignment with your true, God-given identity. The first is who

God says you are. Very good (Genesis 1:31), healed (Isaiah 53:5), chosen (John 15:16), redeemed (Hebrews 9:15). The second is what God has told you to do. Fear not (Isaiah 41:10), cast all of your anxiety upon him (1 Peter 5:7), do not be anxious or worried about anything (Philippians 4:6), trust in the Lord with all your heart (Proverbs 3:5). These spiritual identifiers remind you not to misidentify yourself by a condition in your body or by the circumstances in your life, but to consult with and keep your confidence in God always.

Because your mind, body, and spirit are interconnected, each influenced by and influencing the others, your mental and spiritual health can have physical consequences. This means that something that is unseen, such as your thoughts, can produce tangible, visible changes to your body. Emotions such as fear, anxiousness, and worry can cause processes to take place in your body that your body wasn't designed to experience, yet because it fights for you, your body attempts to correct the dysfunction.

This is why an ongoing awareness of God's Word and his desires for you is essential to your physical health and well-being. This doesn't mean that all physical illness is due to some aspect of your spiritual life. This is a reminder about the importance of examining all aspects of who you are in order to expand your understanding of the many ways stress and sickness can appear in your wonderfully made vessel. It's my hope that this reminder also opens your eyes to the many ways healing can take place.

You are not your diagnosis. Because nursing taught me to address a patient by name, I cringe every time I hear someone begin a conversation with their illness or list the hereditary diseases in their family, suggesting that they don't have a fighting chance because of it.

Your identity doesn't change because some condition exists that requires your awareness and care. You don't become the disease simply because its existence requires you to tend to your needs differently and on a deeper level. The condition one faces can take up lots of mental space. It can become a distraction from the things you enjoy and would prefer to give your time and attention to. It can also alter the way you work and the lifestyle you had become accustomed to. But what you cannot do is begin misidentifying yourself because of it.

It's true that you can't choose where you came from, but you can absolutely choose where you're going. Even when you're experiencing an illness, you can take steps toward your healing. Even though others in your family have experienced a disease, it doesn't mean you're doomed to experience it too, so you must refuse to use this as an excuse to not try to improve your chances of healthy, vibrant living.

There are modifiable lifestyle practices—such as the foods you eat, the way you handle stress, the quality of your sleep, your social network, cultural beliefs, and physical activity—that can decrease the chances of experiencing disease and improve the chances of healing what may already be present.

Just like every other aspect of this world, your thoughts, your behaviors, and the characteristics your genes express can be changed. Don't want grandmama's pill case and medicine cabinet to be in your future? There are things you can do to avoid it. Don't want to constantly worry about that disease that impacted half the women in your bloodline? There are things you can do to minimize your chances. Don't want to leave this life prematurely like your loved one? There are options to help extend your life.

It all begins with what you believe. If you're already convinced that you have no chance, chances are you won't behave differently in a way that helps and supports you to achieve your goal of long, healthy living. This belief then becomes an internal limitation, resulting in excuses about why you cannot succeed in changing your health or any other area of your life. And this is less than the ideal God intended.

Now that you know you absolutely do have a fighting chance, what are you going to do about it? You get to choose. You get to influence your thoughts, your health, your lived experience, and add as many healthful practices to your life as possible.

No, my friend. You are not your diagnosis. And to address any remaining concern, let's explore the meaning of a diagnosis. A diagnosis is the process of identifying the nature of a disease, illness, or condition that explains the signs and symptoms. Therefore a diagnosis offers information that can be used to make decisions about your next steps, including the beneficial pathways you can take toward healing as you continue living. A diagnosis gives you the opportunity to find the root cause of whatever you're facing and work to return your body and your being to homeostasis, that state of balance in your body. A diagnosis is not who you are.

Whether you picked up this book and have no signs or symptoms of sickness, or you're already experiencing less-than-ideal health conditions, I'm here to remind you that you're wonderfully made. There are tools that you can take advantage of, and armor that you can protect yourself with, to help you utilize your body for your own benefit and for God's glory.

2

Stress Invasion

DURING ONE OF MY EARLIEST HOSPITAL EXPERIENCES, I needed to take a culture of a wound. The entire experience seemed way too intrusive to me at the time. I couldn't simply wipe the surface of their skin. I had to use a long swab and probe into the deepest parts of the wound, where bacteria could be hiding. After the sample was taken, the swab was labeled and sent off to the lab for testing and identification.

As believers in Christ, we must regularly pause to consider what would be found in us if a culture probed the deepest parts of our lives. An adoption of and passivity to worldly beliefs and practices? Indifference to or acceptance of stress? Festering wounds that you'd rather hold on to than give over to God? I challenge you to probe all the spaces of your life. Examine what's lying around, growing recklessly, causing you undue stress, or unnecessarily deepening the divide between you and your Savior.

Romans 12:2 tells us not to conform to the patterns of this world, not to become so well-adjusted to the culture that we fit in without even thinking. This means that our lives should be labeled, identified, and exhibit traits that are different from the stress and chaos taking place around us, as we do not rely on our own strength, but on the provision of God.

NONCONFORMITY

If you're wondering what to do when you're surrounded by a culture of people, news, and situations that are full of stress and anxiety, and if it seems like you can feel the stress everyone else is feeling, I want to remind you that you don't have to.

Before you ever engage with the world or come in close enough proximity to feel the weight of the stress and suffering that's present, you can turn toward your heavenly Father and seek the antidotes to stress included in our biblical instruction manual.

You can come to Jesus with your weariness and stressful burdens and receive the rest you need (Matthew 11:28). You can cast all of your cares, anxieties, worries, and concerns on him, because you know that no matter what is going on, he deeply cares about you (1 Peter 5:7). You also don't have to be anxious about anything. You can pray and petition, with thanksgiving, presenting your requests to God (Philippians 4:6).

Even when the fear, anxiety, and worries come, and it feels like you and the world are facing one stressful struggle after another, you have an antidote and a Savior you can turn to again and again, helping you to combat stress and persevere in the midst of relentless attempts to be swayed by and saturated with the stress the culture is feeling.

When you trust in the Lord and place your confidence in him, it won't matter which way the culture blows, because your roots are firmly and deeply planted in God, and your ability to relax and experience his peace, comfort, and rest is unshakable.

CULTURAL MYTHS

I was meeting with a group of fellow entrepreneurs who were going to offer feedback on a project I was working on. I'd been looking forward to this meeting for weeks, as I valued the opinions and experience the members had. As I began sharing my desire to teach a course on relaxation, I was abruptly cut off mid-sentence as one of my peers declared that she hated the thought of relaxing because anything less than being constantly on the go would cost her money and make her miserable. Her words stung and left me feeling a bit deflated. I knew that I was supposed to be teaching others how to relax, whether or not the group agreed. So I continued to work on my project, trusting in the instruction and path I was on.

A few months later, in a similar meeting, this same peer revealed to the group that although she loved her work, it was destroying multiple aspects of her personal life, including her health and her marriage. She could no longer keep up with being busy for the sake of feeling productive. She had to slow down, relax, and reconnect in meaningful ways to the parts of her life she'd been neglecting.

If you find yourself staying busy, distracting yourself from what's going on in your life, and avoiding paying attention to how you feel, it will catch up with you eventually. Whether you fear what you'll find in the stillness or have adopted cultural practices that teach you to hustle endlessly, existing in a constant state of busyness, with no break in sight, will increase the amount of stress you experience. This practice of busyness that doesn't allow you to tune in to your needs, dedicate time to the people and things you enjoy, or devote any meaningful time and space to cultivate your relationship with God can be a fatal distraction that keeps you from stopping your stress or the unnecessary fallout busyness can produce in your life.

Have you ever found yourself in situations that are much more than you could bear—some you put yourself in, and others that God put you in? Because sometimes, God will do what's necessary to get your attention and to cause you to rely on him more than yourself. If you're unaware that he's seeking deeper trust and reliance within your relationship, you may miss what God is trying to build between you. So be careful not to measure your strength by the amount of pain you can endure. Your resilience and ability to withstand stress and recover quickly from it can be a worthless badge of honor preventing you from turning toward God and putting your complete trust in him. Equally as dangerous is the practice of blindly following false narratives that have no biblical foundation, such as God won't give you more than you can bear. Not only is this not true, but it also causes you to continuously try to rely on yourself, believing that you're stronger than you are, which will inevitably lead to more stress.

CULTURAL DISCERNMENT

The next time you see the rise and widespread use of a term or other influential information, take a moment to discern what's being said and if the message actually applies to you.

Let's use toxic positivity as an example. Although this is a type of coping mechanism in which one suppresses negative emotions, the term has also been used to discredit those living positive, joyful lives; those who exhibited resilience; and those who have developed an optimistic outlook on life.

When this type of cultural behavior occurs, you need to ask yourself, again using toxic positivity as our example: Am I truly exhibiting a negative coping mechanism, only displaying positive emotions and suppressing the negative ones? Or are others seeing my light and can't seem to handle how brightly I'm shining?

Because in this example, being positive doesn't necessarily mean you dismiss stressful, tragic, or painful experiences. For many, it means that even in the midst of difficult times, you know who's keeping you, where your help is coming from, and that no matter what you're facing, you still win!

In John 15:9-11, we see that if we remain in Jesus' love by being obedient and keeping his commandments, we can experience and enjoy an intimate, loving relationship with him like he experiences with his Father. And in spite of external circumstances, we are assured and maintain our confidence because we know that God is in control, and walking in his ways enables us to experience fullness of joy.

So if you find that the culture is wielding its influence as a weapon, attempting to shun or shame you for being who you are even after all that you've been through, you need to challenge the narrative.

Let me put it like this: Don't you dare dim your light, fall in line, or be devoured by the culture. You stand up and sing praises to God like,

"You don't know what he's done for me. He gave me the victory. I love him. I love him. I really love the Lord." Then boldly, confidently, and unapologetically continue being the light you were sent here to be no matter how the surrounding culture labels you. Know who you are and whose you are, and act accordingly.

And just in case you're wondering, this is one of the reasons why I write. I do this for my culture, to let others know what it looks like to think independently of what has become the norm. To consciously take an unpopular stance, not just in opposition to stress or anything else, but to lovingly redirect false or misleading narratives that attempt to override, ignore, or diminish truth. To ring the alarm and remind you that the Bible is the truth you're meant to be consuming, not whatever clever scheme the culture serves up to you each day.

MASKED BY MEDICINE

I cringe every time a medication commercial comes on, many of which play on the fears of those watching them. Sure, medication can be helpful and, in some cases, absolutely necessary. But medicine isn't always designed to fix the problem, often masking the signs and symptoms of what's being experienced.

When the body is seeking a solution, it alarms you, letting you know that something is going on and needs your attention. The problem, however, doesn't go away because medicine is taken. So the body will keep alarming until the pain, dysfunction, imbalance, or wound is healed or encapsulated—until the body has had enough time to wrap scar tissue around an area, form a blood clot to stop the bleeding, regenerate cut nerves, or replenish the vitamin, mineral, water, or sleep it lacks.

Many medicines don't heal the pain; they dampen your awareness of it. Many medicines don't replenish deficiencies; the body finds a way to work around the problem, continually alarms you of the problem, or begins to function at a lesser capacity than intended.

This is why pain usually seems worse after initial doses of medication wear off, or blood pressure skyrockets after missing a few pills, or insomnia reappears after a sedative is discontinued. This rebound effect demonstrates that the cause of the condition being masked by medicine is still present, but either your perception of it has decreased, or the medication has brought it into a normal range.

But just like the alarm clock after you hit snooze, your body will set off the alarm again. The longer you take to address the alarm directly by turning it off, the louder and more disturbing it becomes. This opens one up to dependency on whatever medication initially relieved the stress or condition, or to addiction, with many searching for something stronger to alleviate their pain.

So whether the medicine being taken is legal or illegal, over-the-counter or prescribed, a preventive measure or pain reliever, it's likely to do what is intended: numb or distract your mind from the condition for a while. But we must not stop there or become satisfied with the temporary result. Seeking the fullness of healing should always be our goal.

Now, let me be clear. If your blood pressure or sugar is out of a healthy range, take the medicine. If your pain is debilitating and keeps you from normal daily function or the ability to work or play, you may need to take some form of medicine. The point isn't to avoid medicine completely, but to have a full understanding about what the medicine is, what its side effects are, and what you need to actively be doing to create conditions that enable your body to heal and restore as much of its natural functioning as possible.

Knowing and understanding that there are different types of medicine and medical practices, including different philosophies that drive each practice, is significant when it comes to your own health and healing. Your ability to discern what to use, when to use it, and who to consult regarding your care can make all the difference in your life, healing, and longevity.

It's also critical that we understand that as the body of Christ, we're not exempt from suffering, and we needn't attempt to mask any spiritual strongholds or difficulties that we're going through. We must ask ourselves if we're unwilling to leave behind harmful thought patterns, sins, or ways of the world that go against God's will. Because like weeds, these sins and strongholds will remain and begin to suffocate you, competing for the attention meant to be given to God, releasing toxins in your life, and damaging the spiritual fruit your life should exhibit.

God already knows what we're experiencing anyway. He waits for us to turn to him because he is the solution and antidote for everything we're dealing with. He desires to be present with us in every circumstance instead of being overlooked for any form of subpar, idol medicine.

God has also provided us with help through other people. In Galatians 6:2 we're commanded to carry each other's burdens, and in Ecclesiastes 4:9-10 we're reminded that two are better than one because someone who falls down can be helped back up by the other. This means that we shouldn't attempt to mask what we're going through from others; hiding will cause our problems to persist, and we will likely remain down longer than necessary.

Ignoring, suppressing, or refusing to share what's distressing you—whether it's an act of masking, avoidance, or denial—are all unbeneficial coping mechanisms that can heighten your stress and anxiety.

Additional examples of unbeneficial and harmful coping mechanisms include smoking, drinking, drug use, gambling, overeating, undereating, isolating, self-harm, negative self-talk, doom scrolling, impulsive spending, or catastrophizing. These can be lifestyle practices that have been modeled or are easily accessible and adopted, but they're usually difficult to stop, adding yet another layer of stress and masking to one's life that requires more healing.

TRAUMATIC EVENTS

There was a call from the emergency room, and the person on the other end of the phone told us to be ready for a potential car crash victim. When an accident occurs and the injuries are severe, all departments that may need to participate in the care of the patient are notified to stand by to assist.

As my colleagues went to prep the operating room, I was asked to go to the ER to be the eyes and ears for this case, relaying any pertinent information back to the department so they could prepare the appropriate instruments and supplies for the surgeons.

When I arrived at the emergency room, the patient, who was being transported by helicopter, had not yet arrived. Similar preparations were being made in this department, with various personnel standing by to assist.

When the patient was wheeled through the doors, CPR was being administered by the paramedics, and continued once the patient had entered the ER bay. The patient was intubated. Chest tubes were inserted. Though there were no visible external injuries, the extensive internal damage caused such severe stress to the body that recovery was impossible.

In situations like these, stress causes a ripple effect. The injured person is instantly impacted. Those who work tirelessly in an attempt to resuscitate and stabilize the patient are impacted as they exhaust their knowledge, physical efforts, and empathy. And the families, who had no idea that their loved one would not return home that day, experience a permanent life-changing event. When these sudden and traumatically stressful events occur, they don't allow you to stop your stress. There is no warning. No way to prepare. And the result is the end of life as they knew it. A new reality must be faced without the person they loved, accompanied by an abrupt wave of stress.

INVISIBLE TRAUMA

Fatal internal injuries like that crash victim's are some of the most disheartening experiences I've witnessed as a nurse. Traumatic brain injuries, overdoses that people never woke up from. There's something about the individual not showing visible signs of illness or injury that can make acceptance of that truth extremely difficult, and living that reality, debilitating.

Unfortunately, so many people we know, love, and interact with every day are also suffering from their own forms of invisible trauma. Deeply rooted pain that the eye simply cannot see. They get up day after day bearing the weight of their wounds, unwilling, unable, or unaware that healing is possible and can be worked on.

When the stress experienced by trauma piles on top of every other stress that's already present, life can feel like too much to handle, causing those experiencing invisible trauma to break—mentally, physically, emotionally, or spiritually—and the overflow of pain causes even more damage in their lives.

Invisible trauma develops in many ways, from various forms of abuse and neglect, to being routinely overlooked, ignored, or invalidated. Because they were never meant to endure the stress and trauma they witnessed or experienced, they must also deal with varying degrees of self-directed shame, judgment, criticism, hopelessness, and the protective responses that arise such as defensiveness, dissociation, and distress.

SHOCK

I was asked to remove a patient's bandages and prep her head for surgery. She had also been in a car crash, and I was unaware of the extent of her injuries, but I knew that her head required some stitches. When I removed the last piece of gauze, her true injury was revealed, and her curiosity took over. She kept reaching up attempting to touch the part of her that was bandaged at the accident scene. And I kept reminding her that she needed to put her hands down. She wanted to touch her wounds because no one had told her what condition she was in. She felt normal because of the amount of adrenaline coursing through her body and was convinced that her injury couldn't possibly be that bad as she was wide awake and not in that much pain.

Sometimes, though, you're wounded so badly that shock has left you unaware of all the damage that's taken place. Other people can see your wounds, your trauma, your need for help, and all you can do is continue grasping for answers about what happened to you in the process of your trauma. Stress infiltrates your life, but because you're in a state of shock and automatic protective mechanisms have taken over, you become numb to the extent of your injuries.

Whether or not your trauma is visible to the naked eye, God sees you, and knows exactly what you're going through. As you observe your stress and take note of the signs and symptoms you're witnessing in your own life, you'll become better equipped to partner with him in healing your stress.

3

Signs and Symptoms of Stress

SHE WORE A FLOOR-LENGTH COAT AS she walked circles around our local mall. Her coat was so distinct, like nothing I'd ever seen before, and her graceful stride made her presence even more distinct. I was a new mother, determined to get some exercise and potentially engage with other adults. So every morning, I got up, placed my smiling baby in the stroller, and went to walk the mall as well. Every day we'd smile and wave as we walked by one another. One of the familiar faces I'd grown accustomed to looking for.

A few years went by. I had more babies, and less interest in packing everyone up to brave the unpredictable, and often unproductive, attempt at a daily walk. Yet some faces and encounters leave such an impression that they're practically unforgettable.

The next time I saw her, I was hurriedly loading my groceries into my SUV. She was slumped over a bit as she held the arm of a grocery store employee, and I was taken aback. This was not her usual stride, and her face didn't hold the same smile. Something was happening, and everyone in that parking lot seemed to notice, except for the employee. "Oh, this happens all the time," he said as he continued walking her to her car. Several of us tried to stop him, telling him not to let her get in the car. "She's having a medical emergency!" we shouted at him. But he was completely unaware. He was used to helping people to their cars and seemed to take pride in his efforts.

But what happened next seemed to unfold so fast. She backed out of the parking spot so quickly that she didn't seem to notice the people banging on her door trying to get her to stop. But by this time, she had hit the accelerator, driving dangerously fast toward a building. I grabbed my phone and called 911, reporting the emergency in hopes that she and those around her would remain safe, and she would get the care that she needed.

The woman standing next to me asked me if I was all right. We were all startled by what had taken place, and she saw what I didn't even realize was happening: the tears were streaming down my face. "You know her?" she asked. At that moment, I simply said yes. I didn't know her personally. I couldn't tell you her name. But I did know that this was not her normal behavior. I did know that the way her body moved and the expression on her face were not typical for her.

I also knew that this employee's kind gesture, coupled with his lack of knowledge, could have caused catastrophic damage. He didn't know he was holding on to someone in need of medical attention. He thought this was just another day on the job.

Today, I'm privileged to have your attention, and just in case you are unaware of the gravity of your situation, I want you to know that it's highly likely that the stress you're experiencing is quite dangerous. Just as I didn't hesitate to report that emergency, I won't hesitate to tell you that it's time to get the help you need. It's time to stop whatever you're doing, pay attention to the stress in your life, and eliminate it before something catastrophic and irreversible happens. In order to do that, though, you must become aware of the signs and symptoms of stress in your own life.

AWAKEN TO THE STRESS YOU'RE EXPERIENCING

Noticing stress can be as simple as having an awareness that something just isn't right, feels off, unpleasant, you're not where you want to be, or you don't feel how you want to feel. Noticing can take time if you're dealing with thoughts, feelings, and ideas that stress is normal or necessary. If you're in a situation that you believe you're supposed to be in and don't honor your power of choice to change, walk away from, or enhance the situation, you'll continue to experience the stress until your perspective changes. Are the headaches you've been regularly experiencing a result of stress? Are the negative thoughts you've been ruminating on caused by stress? Simply noticing can be the key to shifting away from stress.

I began to notice that whenever I was on call, I'd turn my pager up to full volume before I'd fall asleep each night because I was afraid that I'd sleep right through the alarm. I deeply regretted this choice as the repetitive beeping rang out in the darkness, seemingly rattling the walls of my apartment and my heart. The pager, a device used as a dispatch for help, would send me into my own tailspin as I'd tumble out of bed struggling to catch my breath and find my shoes.

My alarming pager indicated that an emergency surgery was necessary within the hour. It also acted as a lifeline for the patient in need of care and the operating room skeleton crew awaiting some assistance. But for me, the pager had become a stressor, a reason to remain alert and on guard for hours in anticipation of responding to any form of trauma. When I was on call, I could never quite get comfortable. I anxiously awaited the page that would suspend whatever I was doing, or the clock to signal the end of my shift, whichever came first, and it left me on edge. Although I loved the work, this little device seemed to take me out of my element, leaving me a distressed version of my normal self. Yet noticing how I felt when I was on call gave me the opportunity to change my perspective.

Whenever I'd feel too overwhelmed by that little device, I'd think about the man I met at my first volunteer position in a hospital. He was a volunteer too and had a beaming personality and striking blond hair. He also had a distinctly large abdomen, the result of liver failure. He was on the transplant list, volunteering at the hospital so that he was never too far away from the place that could change his life. He happily wore his pager day and night. His pager wasn't a stressor to him. He was hoping for a miracle, and the thought of his pager going off meant a chance for a new, healthier life. He didn't view it as cumbersome or lie awake in a panic for fear that it would go off. Quite the opposite. His pager was a welcome accessory.

You see, that's the thing about stressors. They're subjective. What's stressful to me, you may ignore or even laugh at. While what's stressful to you may have never been on my radar, let alone a concern.

So how do we begin to understand stress when the fundamental aspects of what we find stressful are vastly different? We start by following the sequence of events that any stressor causes in the body. Because no matter what you or I perceive to be stressful, the exact same thing occurs within our bodies when faced with a stressor.

YOUR STRESS RESPONSE

Anything that you perceive as a threat, any stimulus that causes you stress, is a stressor. The psychological and biological changes you experience upon encountering a stressor are what constitute the stress response, a complex entanglement of nervous, endocrine, and immune systems that begins in the amygdala.[1] The amygdala is an area of the brain that contributes to emotional processing and constantly interprets external sights and sounds.

When a threat is perceived, the amygdala sends a signal to the hypothalamus, an area of the brain that functions like a command center. The hypothalamus then communicates with the rest of the body through the autonomic nervous system, which consists of two components—the sympathetic nervous system and the parasympathetic nervous system—that control involuntary functions such as heart rate, blood pressure, and breathing.

When the hypothalamus activates the sympathetic nervous system by sending signals to the autonomic nerves in the adrenal glands, the adrenal glands release adrenaline, also called epinephrine, into the bloodstream. The circulation of epinephrine throughout the body causes numerous physiological changes. Breathing rate, heart rate, pulse, and blood pressure increase. Blood sugar, or glucose, and fats already stored within the body are released, attempting to supply the body with more energy. Extra oxygen is sent to the brain in an attempt to increase alertness. And all of this takes place in the blink of an eye before you're even aware that it's happening.

If a threat is still perceived by the time the original surge of epinephrine subsides, the hypothalamus activates the second phase of the stress response, initiating a chain reaction of hormones throughout the endocrine system, keeping the body on high alert. If the threat comes to an end, cortisol levels fall and the parasympathetic nervous system calms the body down, suppressing the stress response.

If the threat doesn't end, the body exists in a state of crisis, and when the body is in crisis, it will switch into survival mode. When one is in survival mode, being exposed to repeated or chronic stress, this leads to allostatic load, the cumulative wear and tear taking a toll on the entire body. High allostatic load increases the risk of poor health outcomes, including cardiovascular disease, diabetes, severe mood problems, and higher rates of mortality. And when one's allostatic load becomes their health baseline, they can begin to exhibit symptoms of crisis fatigue, a type of burnout experienced with prolonged stress. Crisis fatigue symptoms include exhaustion, mental detachment, a sense of hopelessness, grief, hormone imbalances, weight gain, and aches and pains.

The body's normal metabolic processes produce free radicals, but when our cells are unable to keep up with detoxifying them and they build up, this excess causes oxidative stress, which damages cells, proteins, and DNA, triggers inflammation, alters signaling pathways, and can increase the risk of cancer.

Our world continuously attempts to normalize stress and busyness, preventing us from reaching a full state of surrender, and confusing us about whether we can even attain a life with less stress. That's why it's critical that as a believer in Christ, you understand how your body is formed and how it functions so that you can take care of it to the best of your ability. Your body, being the wisdom-laced ecosystem that it is, is programmed to do everything in its power to heal and sustain your life. Yet your body and your overall health are directly impacted by your choices, especially the stress-filled ones. Your choices will ultimately override and steer your body in the direction you choose to take it.

So whether you're bombarded by daily stress or barely notice the subtle stress that's present, when stressed becomes your chronic state, it contributes to an abundance of stress-related health problems. Let's travel the body, system by system, uncovering the ways stress infiltrates and erodes your physical being.

Integumentary system. Your integumentary system consists of your skin, hair, and nails. Your skin is your largest organ and often reflects what's happening inside your body. Stress makes your skin more sensitive and reactive. It slows down wound healing, which negatively impacts preexisting skin conditions.[2] When you're under stress, your glands produce more oil, which can worsen acne-prone skin. The inflammation that stress causes can exacerbate conditions like eczema, psoriasis, atopic and contact dermatitis, and alopecia areata. And stress hormones can accelerate the damage and loss of elastin and collagen, the proteins responsible for the elasticity and firmness of the skin. This interference then causes an increase in fine lines and wrinkles.

Stress can also contribute to hair thinning and hair loss as the release of cortisol impacts and disrupts the proper functioning of the dermal papilla of the hair follicle, which is responsible for regulating the frequency of hair follicle regeneration and the characteristics of the hair shaft. Stress disturbs the hair cycle, causing hair follicles to prematurely enter a resting phase, so that new strands of hair aren't produced. Stress can also cause the premature graying of hair by quickly depleting melanocyte stem cells, which are responsible for regenerating hair pigment.

Stress makes it more difficult for your body to absorb the vitamins and minerals necessary for strong, healthy nails, resulting in nail pitting, ridging, and shredding as side effects of your weakened nails. Stress can also cause slow nail growth or brittle and easily broken nails.

Muscular system. With the sudden presence of stress, the body attempts to guard against pain and injury by contracting and tensing up your muscles. This tension takes great energy, reduces circulation, decreases the absorption of nutrients by the muscles, and increases inflammation. Prolonged stress can lead to soreness, tightness, pain, and muscle spasms. Stress can also cause premature decline of muscle strength.

Your tense muscles can cause back, neck, and shoulder pain, headaches, body aches, and a tightened pelvic floor, which can lead to constipation, urgency, pelvic pain, and painful sex.

Skeletal system. The cortisol released because of your stress response causes an increase in bone resorption. When stress is prolonged, the calcium depletion cannot be replaced fast enough by your diet, so your body is constantly being stripped of calcium. This can lead to porous, brittle bones and eventually osteoporosis.

The inflammation caused by stress can damage cartilage, tendons (which attach muscles to bones), and ligaments (which hold joints together), leading to conditions such as arthritis, tendonitis, and osteoarthritis.

Nervous system. Stress activates the sympathetic nervous system, signaling the adrenal glands, which are a part of the endocrine system, to release adrenaline and cortisol. If the central nervous system doesn't return to a normal state or the stressor continues, the stress response and ongoing release of stress hormones will continue. This can cause you to become hypervigilant, anxious, and always on high alert.

Endocrine system. The endocrine system releases cortisol in response to stress. When high levels of cortisol come in contact with your body's tissues for extended periods of time, some tissue and cellular alterations can occur. Excess circulating fat and fat stores can be relocated and deposited centrally on the body, deep in the abdomen. This is where obesity is likely to begin. Along with the increase in adipose tissue comes an increase in the hormones produced and released by the adipose tissue, including leptin, a hormone that influences appetite and fat storage and regulates the balance between food intake and energy expenditure.[3] When leptin levels are too high in your body, you can become leptin resistant. This means your brain no longer responds to leptin as it normally would, and you don't get the sensation of feeling full. High levels of leptin can then lead to nonalcoholic fatty liver disease, depression, food addiction, and neurodegenerative disorders such as Parkinson's and Alzheimer's disease.

Additional endocrine disorders such as diabetes, gonadal dysfunction, hyperthyroidism, and Graves' disease can also occur as a result of stress, as well as a thyroid storm, when your thyroid releases large amounts of hormone in a short time.[4] This rare but possible complication of hyperthyroidism is a life-threatening medical emergency. Stress can also cause an adrenal crisis, another life-threatening condition in which your adrenal glands don't make enough cortisol.[5]

Digestive system. The digestive system cannot properly function with too much stress. Stress can cause a range of gastrointestinal problems including inflammation, bloating, cramping, and loss of appetite. Stress impedes the flow of digestion, delaying the emptying of the stomach, which can lead to nausea, heartburn, indigestion, and stomachache. As stress slows down the stomach, it increases function in the large intestine, which can lead to bowel or urinary urgency or diarrhea. Chronic stress can contribute to ulcers and irritable bowel syndrome.

Lymphatic system. Recent studies suggest that chronic stress activates a neuroinflammatory signaling pathway. This alters lymphatic structures and increases lymph flow, allowing tumor cells to spread and accelerating metastasis, leading to poor cancer survival.[6]

Cardiovascular system. Stress can cause spasms in the blood vessels of the heart, increase inflammation in the arteries, and cause instability in the heart's electrical conduction system. Long-term stress and the resulting high levels of cortisol can increase blood pressure, blood cholesterol, blood sugar, and triglycerides, which are all common risk factors for heart disease, heart attacks, and stroke. Chronic stress is believed to increase the risk of coronary artery disease by accelerating the rate of atherosclerosis.

Respiratory system. As the airway between the nose and lungs constricts due to stress, respiratory symptoms such as rapid breathing or shortness of breath can occur. Hyperventilation, asthma attacks, coughing, or an increase in mucus can also result from stress-induced respiratory problems. Breathing faster, yet less efficiently, can lower your oxygen levels, triggering you to breathe even faster in an effort to get the oxygen your body needs.

If a foreign particle such as smoke, fungi, exhaust, dust, viruses, or bacteria is the stressor impacting the lungs, inflammation can occur, which could eventually lead to scar tissue in the lungs. And difficulty breathing can often leave one prone to panic attacks.

Female reproductive system. High levels of ongoing stress impact the brain's ability to produce and regulate key hormones. When hormone levels are unbalanced, your menstrual cycle can be affected, leading to delayed or missed periods, amenorrhea, and a flow that is lighter or heavier than normal. Because your pH balance is sensitive, stress can easily throw it off, causing conditions like yeast infections or bacterial vaginosis, a vaginal infection that requires antibiotics.

Chronic stress can also impact fertility, disrupting the production of hormones or the signal to the ovaries to release an egg each month, causing anovulation or delayed ovulation.[7] High levels of stress hormones can also impact the likelihood of successful implantation and one's ability to maintain pregnancy, as well as fetal development.

Male reproductive system. Inflammation caused by chronic stress can cause structural and functional damage of the male reproductive tract.[8] Chronic stress can also affect testosterone production, resulting in a decline in libido, and interfere with spermatogenesis, the development of mature sperm, reducing sperm quantity, quality, and motility. Chronic stress may also lead to impotence.

Immune system. Unlike other organ systems, the immune system provides surveillance to all tissues of the body. Your immune system is a network of white blood cells, organs, and antibodies that work together to protect you against germs and foreign invaders such as viruses, bacteria, fungi, and parasites. The stress-related hormones connected to chronic stress can cause low-grade, persistent inflammation, suppressing and dysregulating immune responses and disrupting the number, function, and receptivity of immunoprotective cells, all of which can result in illness.[9]

Whew! I know that was a lot to absorb. So take a deep breath in. Now lean in and let me ask you something. Is it just me, or does it seem like the objective of stress is to steal, kill, and destroy? And if this is the case, stress is also attempting to snatch your sound mind, spiritual security, abundant life, and attention to the Shepherd. It's no wonder that, even for the believer, experiencing stress can leave one feeling scattered, bound, and unsafe. Stress is a slow poison contributing to your daily deterioration and deliberate demise.

WHAT CAN YOU DO ABOUT THE STRESS YOU'RE EXPERIENCING?

Increasing your awareness and understanding of when and how stress affects you can help you put an end to it. For example, if you know heavy traffic on your commute to work stresses you out, you may decide to leave earlier, or try out new routes with less traffic in order to avoid an unnecessary stress response. Do you experience more stress early in the day or in the evening? Are there certain times of the year that feel more stressful to you than others?

If you don't enjoy public speaking, your neck and shoulders may get tense before you have to do a presentation at work, indicating a stress response. If you experience abdominal pain after eating a high-fat meal, your body may be exhibiting a stress response in an attempt to communicate its reaction to what you've eaten. Do you scroll through social media or TV mindlessly when you're experiencing stress? Do you overeat or attempt to numb the stress in other ways? There are always clues, subtle or overt, that are trying to guide you away from your stressors. Recognizing when and how you experience stress will open your awareness to them.

Next, focus on the stress that you can change. Major causes of stress are feelings of hopelessness, disempowerment, and frustration. These particular emotions can arise when we are continuously exposed to problems and challenges that seem insurmountable, like moral dilemmas and social injustices. News media will expose you to these constantly. And if you're not careful, you can get sucked into a continuous cycle of despair.

Sometimes, however, there's nothing you can do about the thing that's causing you a stress reaction. You can't get out of your car and move the overturned truck blocking your path and preventing you from getting to work on time. So you have to release what you can't change. It can be difficult to admit that we're unable to control, effectively change, or improve every situation we face. But the reality is we can't. Releasing ourselves of the responsibility to do so and letting go of our expectations for things to be a certain way can help us get rid of stress.

You get to choose how you'll respond to stress and things out of your control. You can reduce the stress response, reframe your view of the stressor, and take control of your internal environment. You can take a moment to pray for the driver and others who are potentially going to be late to their destinations. You can call into work and explain what's happening so they're aware of your situation instead of pushing on the horn trying to scare others out of your way. You can turn on some music and praise God that you weren't involved in the accident.

David, who faced many stressful events including political turmoil, enemies, and personal failures, often turned to God for comfort and guidance. In 2 Samuel 22:7 David says, "In my distress I called to the LORD; I called out to my God. From his temple he heard my voice; my cry came to his ears." We too can respond by turning to God with our stress, failures, turmoil, and the things that are simply out of our control.

Because when you respond to stress in ways that aren't helpful, you begin to develop a defeatist attitude, regularly filled with worry and negativity. And this can make it very difficult to practically handle stress. Taking steps to transform these attitudes can radically alter what previously felt insurmountable.

Approaching each situation as a challenge, instead of a threat, eliminates the stress response and gives you a greater ability to focus, have clarity about what's taking place, and remain in control. So when you're tempted to allow stressful events to dictate your attitude, know that there's always a way of escape, even off of the stress cycle.

MORE SUPPORT

I've been a nurse for long enough to know that things aren't always as simple as one, two, three. I'm also aware that there are those who have settled for and become comfortable with mediocrity, which doesn't serve anyone, including the kingdom of God. Your ability to discern, be self-aware, and know what applies to you and your condition is critical to your health and healing. Be honest with yourself about what you do and don't need, and move forward with optimizing your health in mind. If you know that you have a real need for support, be it through therapy, medication, or invasive procedure, you should explore those options and do all that you can to heal. These options may significantly decrease your stress or help you recalibrate, so that you can take further action toward your health and healing.

Stress should always be taken into consideration by a health care provider. Yet because stress is personal, subjective, and can't be measured from one person to the next, it may be difficult for others to understand its impact on your life. Not being heard, believed, or supported when you know something is going on in your life or body is terrible to experience. Understand that I see you, believe you, and encourage you to seek a second and a third opinion when necessary, sharing as much background information as necessary with the right care provider in an effort to transform your life and restore your health. In case you're in need of additional support, I've included some resources for you at the back of this book.

WILLINGNESS TO HEAL

The patient's wound was long, about eight inches or so, and ran between her knee and hip on the outer aspect of her thigh. The wound was infected and in need of debridement, which is another way of saying the infected area wasn't healing and that tissue needed to be removed. The opened area had been tightly packed with gauze, and I had just been informed that I would be the one removing the gauze from the wound.

Although I knew this procedure would help the progression of her healing, I didn't want to touch it. It looked so painful, and the thought of causing her more pain by cleaning the wound out didn't sit well with me. But what choice did I have? Leaving the gauze inside her thigh, or the wound open indefinitely, wasn't an option. This was part of the healing process, and I was there to help her through it.

Before I began, I couldn't have imagined how deep the wound was, or what it contained. I also couldn't have imagined how uncomfortable, and in some moments, downright painful the procedure must've been for the patient. Yet she continued to say, "Don't worry, honey. It has to be done."

My friend, I don't know how long your stress-filled wounds have been with you, how deep and dirty they are, or what parts of you are dying because of them, but I want you to know that facing them and cleaning them out offer you a path to healing that can prevent further damage, stimulate new growth, and bring a new level of freedom to your existence.

4

The Relaxation Remedy

DURING A CLINICAL ROTATION for my master's degree program, I was assigned to the pediatric unit of the hospital. One of the most memorable and transformative experiences during that time was visiting a young patient with scoliosis. As I entered the room with the nurse I was shadowing at the time, the patient was lying in traction on the bed, noticeably agitated and in pain. The nurse didn't offer me too much insight into what she was about to do, but she had what seemed to be a quiet confidence about her. In retrospect, I also believe she was deeply in tune with what was taking place and offering this patient her healing presence.

She walked to their bedside, turned on some soft music, and slowly, intentionally began moving her hands in front of the patient's body. After a few minutes, the agitation subsided, the beating of the heart monitor slowed, and the patient seemed to fall into a deep sleep.

I had never witnessed such a thing before and wanted to know exactly what had taken place. Everything in the space seemed to calm down, including me and the family members. It was such a serene experience.

The nurse described what I had witnessed as healing touch, an energy therapy that uses gentle hand techniques to accelerate healing of the mind, body, and spirit. This was my introduction to holistic nursing and the numerous holistic practices that could disrupt stressful reactions and support the healing and harmony of the whole person.

Why did this matter? At that point in my career, my time was spent caring for patients in the operating room. Some too sick or too injured to ever leave those rooms to live another day. Others presumably went on with their lives, yet they left with scars that would forever remind them of what had taken place. Those patients and experiences also left imprints on me.

The daily witnessing of illness, the excision of disease, and the loss of one's ability to consciously make one's own decisions under the influence of anesthesia was becoming disturbing to me.

I struggled to watch patient after patient be wheeled through those OR doors, as I wondered if they would be better served if we could reach them sooner, teaching preventive care measures—the things you can do before getting sick—wellness strategies, and stress relief practices. Although there will always be a need for medical and surgical care, I wanted to participate in the type of health care that could significantly slow, or completely prevent, disease and its progression.

I wanted to remind others not to get confused by messages that describe our sinful nature, corruptible bodies, and the desires of the flesh that are contrary to the Spirit, because although these things are true, they do not diminish the masterful workmanship that is the physical human body. They do not give us a green light to neglect our bodies simply because this is not our final destination or form. They don't suggest that we should disconnect from these bodies and what they're communicating to us, which then prevents us from glorifying God in our body or deepening the connection with the Holy Spirit within us. And they don't require us to repeatedly degrade our bodies in an attempt to acknowledge our personal awareness of their potential for sin. Our bodies are indeed integral to God's mission here on earth and necessary for us to reflect his glory and share his message so that others too can be saved. Because our neglect, disconnection, and degradation of our body dishonors God and disregards the sacrifice Jesus made to restore humanity's relationship with God through his death on the cross.

As I longed for answers that resembled what I knew to be true of God and how he created us, I studied the Word of God and holistic practices. I began to find alternatives to the medical and surgical interventions I was accustomed to and techniques used to care for those who were already experiencing varying stages of sickness and disease. I also found information that affirmed that our bodies are inherently good, designed to heal, and immeasurably valuable. Although wounds to our bodies are inevitable, we don't have to live fearful of an existence riddled with infirmities and malfunctions because these wounds don't have the last word.

Where you stand determines what you see, and although I stood and worked alongside brilliant, highly skilled, innovative physicians, nurses, and surgical technicians each day, my focus remained on the Great Physician, filtering my vision and furthering my belief that healing and sustained health are obtainable.

You see, God always gives us options. Just like day and night, good and evil, life and death, blessing and cursing, stress too has an opposite, and it's called relaxation.

Relaxation is woven into the fabric of your mind, body, and spirit as the natural antidote to stress, and when it's activated, you experience the relaxation response. Countering everything that stress does, the relaxation response offers you a way of experiencing, expressing, and existing with a relaxed mind, body, and spirit.

I believe the relaxation response exemplifies our original state and relationship with God, a reflection of our unbroken communion with him, full of peace, trust, and unhindered communication.

Yet even after the fall, we still have access to our relaxation response, a physical function and an intentional posture we have the capacity to choose each and every day.

THE RELAXATION RESPONSE

The relaxation response enables us to counteract the sympathetic nervous system's stress response that triggers the release of adrenaline and cortisol and a cascade of problematic processes in the body, responding instead with the parasympathetic nervous system's relaxation response, calming the body and suppressing the stress response.

The relaxation response is the opposite of fight, flight, freeze, and fawn—the various reactions associated with the stress response. It's characterized by a decrease in heart rate, breathing rate, blood pressure, metabolism, and brain activity. Because the brain operates with less strain when we're in a relaxed state, it becomes more efficient in its activity. This results in an increase in alertness, attention, and the decision-making functions of the brain and changes in gene activity opposite those associated with stress.

An increase in relaxation decreases inflammation throughout the body. The body's natural healing processes are activated when we're relaxed, which creates internal conditions that make it easier for our body to repair itself and results in several other benefits. Again, let's look at the body, system by system, to see how relaxation improves our physical being.

Integumentary system. Relaxation minimizes skin inflammation and decreases reactivity of the skin. It also relaxes the muscular tension responsible for wrinkles and slows skin aging. Relaxation improves blood flow to the skin, increasing the nourishment of hair cells, and potentially reducing hair loss. Relaxation also improves circulation, supporting healthier nail growth.

Muscular system. Relaxation decreases muscle tension, muscle pain, and soreness. It also increases blood flow to your muscles, strengthens muscles associated with flexibility and balance, and improves range of motion.

Skeletal system. Relaxation decreases the risk of osteoporosis, encourages better posture, and increases bone density.

Nervous system. Relaxation slows down the autonomic nervous system, enhances function of the nervous system, and activates the parasympathetic nervous system.

Endocrine system. Relaxation reduces the release and impact of stress hormones, such as adrenaline and cortisol. It stimulates the production of endorphins, the body's natural painkillers and mood elevators, reduces the risk of diabetes, and stabilizes insulin secretion.

Digestive system. Relaxation improves digestion, reduces cravings, and enhances the absorption of vitamins and minerals. It also helps to decrease problems like cramping and bloating.

Lymphatic system. Relaxation helps lymph move through the lymphatic system, improves drainage and circulation, and reduces swelling.

Cardiovascular system. Relaxation decreases the risk of heart attack and stroke, decreases heart rate, and lowers blood pressure.

Respiratory system. Relaxation slows the breathing rate, enables deep breaths to be taken naturally, allows for a regular respiration pattern, and increases oxygen intake.

Female reproductive system. Relaxation reduces pelvic pain and PMS pain. It improves blood flow, which aids in healing following childbirth or surgery. Relaxation also improves pregnancy outcomes such as gestational age at birth, birth weight, and mode of delivery, and reduces the occurrence of postpartum complications.

Male reproductive system. Relaxation improves blood flow and mild erectile dysfunction, and also reduces pelvic pain.

Immune system. Relaxation increases immune function, helps lessen the occurrence of sickness, and increases the rate of recovery.

Did you notice how much shorter these sections are versus those of the stress response? When something, in this case a body's relaxation response, is functioning well and correctly, it's efficient and effective at fulfilling its purpose. Your relaxation response is helping you heal and continuously bringing you into a state of harmony—unlike the never-ending cascade of problems caused by your stress response—so there's simply a lot less to discuss when you're in a relaxed state.

REHABILITATE YOUR RELAXATION RESPONSE

After we've been wounded, whether by stress, surgical incision, or sudden accident, it's our job to continue healing and mending the wound because inevitably, scar tissue will develop and remain with varying degrees of thickness. Breaking up the scar tissue covering our physical wounds helps reduce restriction, stiffness, and pain in the area. And I believe similar recovery can occur for our mental, emotional, and spiritual wounds.

Ephesians 4:18 says, "They are darkened in their understanding and separated from the life of God because of the ignorance that is in them due to the hardening of their hearts." In Hebrews 3, Christians were warned not to harden their hearts in rebellion like the first generation of Israelites, and encouraged to persevere in their faith. In Psalm 95:8, the psalmist urges us to not harden our hearts, to recognize and respond to God's voice, and to remember the great things that God has done. Because when your heart becomes hardened and you lose feeling in your body, your conscience, or your emotions, you are numb to what's going on within and around you, including your stress, God's presence, and his ability to transform what you're going through. Nothing shocks you and nothing sparks you to change the situation. You're essentially trapped behind your wounds. But now that you know there's a remedy, you've got to take off your former way of life and begin deconstructing the scar tissue that's present.

So how exactly do you break up scar tissue? You continue to use the area that was wounded, stretching, flexing, and doing physical therapy to restore mobility in the area. When you do this physically, you're developing a rehabilitation regimen that can promote the growth of new collagen cells, increase blood flow to the area, and in some cases, quickly heal the wound and decrease the appearance of the scar. The same applies to your mind and spirit. You have the opportunity to break up mental and spiritual blockages and strongholds, increasing your ability to operate your sound mind and experience the presence and flow of God in your life, while attempting to heal your wounds quickly and minimize the appearance of any scars.

You are entering a space of renewal for your mind, body, and spirit that will also rehab your relaxation response. You're restoring feeling to the areas of your life that have been injured, stressed, hardened, and numb so that you can exist in the freedom and fullness of the life God gifted you.

Rehabilitation of your relaxation response will occur over time, and requires you to regularly practice relaxing. Your rehabilitation plan should be customized to your needs and abilities to help you regain and maximize functionality of your relaxation response. The more you relax, the more likely you are to release the stress that's been hindering your healing processes, increasing your ability to cultivate internal conditions that'll make it easier for your body to repair itself, optimizing your healing and overall well-being. There are a variety of therapies and practices that can support your relaxation efforts, and we'll cover them throughout the following chapters.

REROUTE YOUR RELAXATION

When an artery in the heart is partially or completely blocked, a coronary artery bypass surgery creates a new path for blood to flow around the blockage. That's what we're going to do for your stress.

We're not pretending that stress isn't present. The stress in your life is real to you, and it may take time for you to sort out some of your stressors, heal from their impact, and eliminate them from your life. In the meantime, know that although stress will come, as you walk through the fire of it, you will not be consumed (Isaiah 43:2), and I'm going to teach you how to reroute your relaxation, creating a new path around what's stressful so that relaxation can flow in your life as you learn to rid yourself of stress.

Rerouting your relaxation begins with creating a relaxation response trigger. For example, when my children were little, I began singing "Jesus Loves Me" to them before nap time. It was a simple way to help them unwind and prepare themselves to rest. After a few days, they'd begin to yawn as soon as I started singing because a trigger had been created, and the song indicated that it was time for a nap. Many years later, we still sing "Jesus Loves Me" at bedtime because its relaxing effect remains.

In order to create a relaxation trigger, you begin with the intention of creating a relaxation response within your body. This can be done with music, like our bedtime song, aromatherapy, prayer, a word, a phrase, a meditation, or an image. Once you select what you're going to focus your attention on, comfortably rest in a quiet place. Close your eyes, relax your muscles, and breathe normally. As you breathe, focus your attention on your word, prayer, image, or whatever you're using to generate your relaxation response. If other thoughts arise, simply allow them to pass as you return to your focus. Practice this exercise once or twice a day for ten to twenty minutes. After you've successfully created a relaxation response trigger, you can expand your practice to include other triggers, such as sitting quietly and drinking a cup of tea, soaking in a bathtub, writing in your journal, doing an art project, or viewing an Instagram feed. Yes, my Instagram feed is intentionally designed with pictures of nature and natural elements to help elicit the relaxation response when you visit my page.

The point is, with time and practice, you can create a relaxation response trigger using whatever practice you'd like. Simply set your intentions, focus, and cultivate your relaxation response.

Drs. Herbert Benson and William Proctor created the Benson-Henry Protocol, which includes a second phase designed to deepen your relaxation response: visualization.[1]

Through the use of mental imagery, you engage healing expectation, belief, and memory.

This practice is geared toward those who are already experiencing an illness, medical condition, or stress and strives to help them remember their wellness by counteracting and uprooting the thoughts, expressions, and influence of illness. Because after someone has been ill, in pain, or stressed, their nerves, the synapses in their brain, and even their genetic responses become programmed to exhibit the problem. The use of visualization following the relaxation response helps to create new nerve connections, reversing the illness process and rewiring healing and wellness.

The visualization phase should begin immediately following the relaxation response triggering practice and requires about ten minutes to complete. Visualize yourself in the most peaceful setting of your choosing, free of your illness, pain, or stress; using a measure of faith, begin to expect and believe that your healing is possible.

YOUR SELF-CARE ROUTINE

One way to implement and maintain your relaxation practice is to incorporate it into your self-care routine. Unfortunately, because of its subjective nature, self-care can be misunderstood. In nursing, we always assess one's desire and ability to practice self-care because it's viewed as vital to your health, healing, and overall well-being. So let's go ahead and address three common myths regarding self-care.

The first myth I often encounter is that self-care is selfish. Although one can overindulge in self-care, the practice of taking care of yourself is necessary for a healthy existence. Taking time to care for yourself helps you to remain aware of what's going on in your life, what aspect of your health needs to be tended to, and how you can cultivate deeper healing and relaxation.

The second myth is that self-care is expensive. Although one can choose to spend money on self-care, there are many inexpensive and free activities that can help you to practice self-care, such as going for a walk, listening to music, or reading a book.

The third myth is that self-care takes too much time. It is true that self-care requires an investment of time, but it doesn't have to take hours out of your day. Even a few minutes can make a transformative difference.

Self-care is a foundational element of your well-being, enabling you to get to know yourself better—what you like and dislike, how you function, and what makes you thrive. It's easy to blindly subscribe to other people's best self-care practices, but they may not apply to you. As you regularly care for yourself, you'll learn to honor the things that are best for you and create a plan that makes sense for your lifestyle.

Self-care is not a luxury. It's not something that only those with more time, money, or resources can afford. Self-care is a necessity that enables you to maintain your health, eliminate your stress, and rehabilitate your relaxation response.

Self-care can help you implement non-negotiable aspects of your life, like the number of hours you sleep every night, the type of produce you buy and eat, and the types of exercises you do. It can help you say no to meetings, events, and unnecessary busyness that interfere with your schedule and would potentially decrease the amount of time you can spend relaxing and caring for your well-being.

Self-care will help you see stress coming from a mile away, enabling you to stop it and its harmful effects before they start.

SELF-CARE STRATEGIES

You can honor your own self-care plan by setting boundaries, making space for your self-care practice by blocking off time on your calendar to practice. Pick days and times that you want to have an uninterrupted self-care practice and stick to it. This means making sure that your family and friends are aware of your plans or, at the very least, know you're unavailable when you've scheduled time for self-care. You can also turn off notifications on your devices, set your phone to do-not-disturb, and turn on your out-of-office messages. This will ensure that your time is uninterrupted and you get to focus on your self-care.

You can also optimize your self-care routine and relaxation practice by building a self-care kit. If your life is relatively busy and you find yourself with a few spare moments when you can do something for yourself, you don't want to waste time trying to figure out what to do. Having a self-care kit prepared ahead of time enables you to utilize your time effectively.

With regular relaxation practice, you'll become more aware that your relaxation response has been activated and your practice is working if you feel more relaxed after you've completed a relaxation practice. If you're starting to feel more in control of your stress, feelings, and life than you did before you started your relaxation practice, it's working. If the things that were stressing you before no longer seem to impact you as greatly, again your relaxation practice is working.

You can also begin using a technique called biofeedback to determine if your relaxation practice is benefiting you. Biofeedback helps to determine how relaxed you are using measuring devices to monitor your pulse, blood pressure, temperature, and brain wave patterns.

You can buy a portable blood pressure machine that can tell you your starting heart rate and blood pressure. You can also use a thermometer. Measure your heart rate, blood pressure, or temperature before and after your relaxation practice and write down your results over a thirty-day period. If you're practicing your relaxation response trigger daily, it's likely you'll see your heart rate and blood pressure decreasing over time.

As we process our stress and learn more about our ability to relax throughout this book, I've created a section at the end of the following chapters called "Let's Relax." It includes some questions and Scriptures to ponder as you go, and how-to sections to help guide you in the practical application of relaxation strategies that'll activate your relaxation response. This book isn't solely a message to read; it's one you will want to sit with, process through prayer, work through, and return to. Your application of this content is where you will experience real transformation. I'm thankful to be able to take this journey with you as we trust God to lead us through every word.

5

Respond Holistically

I was working the night shift. There was a rather large and serious operation going on, and the surgeon needed some additional instruments. Our OR was far away from the instrument room, so I ran! He needed those additional tools fast, and I couldn't be the reason why a bad situation got worse. Once I got into the instrument room, I scrambled, searching high and low for the items he asked for. But I couldn't find them. I was desperately looking around, knowing the clock was ticking and that there was no one to call on for help because every person in the department was already in that operating room. Those minutes seemed to go on forever, and I knew I had to make a decision. So I grabbed a cart, placed three different instrument sets on it, and took off down the hall. Although it wasn't exactly what was requested, I knew at least one of the sets would have the instruments that were needed, and we'd figure it out together.

That experience taught me two things. First, no one's coming to save you. You're it! So no matter where you find yourself on the stress and healing spectrum, you've got to utilize the resources and knowledge you have up to this point, make a decision, and move forward believing that things will work out for you. Second, when things are unfamiliar or you're uncertain about what is the best option for a particular situation, grab everything available to you and simply start somewhere. You'll figure out what works and what doesn't when you show up as prepared as you possibly can.

I'm confident you're right where you're meant to be. You've grabbed this book as a resource, which is packed with tools and instruments you can use to lessen your stress and reclaim relaxation. You can take all these resources with you, figuring out what works for you as you go. And the best part about it is, you've got God on your side. He's in the room, the stress, and the chaos with you. You'll figure things out together and restore your relaxation response.

THE HOLISTIC APPROACH

To support the healing of your relaxation response, I recommend that you take a holistic approach, which honors and supports you as the expert of your life experiences; fosters an environment that gives you the tools and space you need to learn, advocate for, and cultivate your own healing and well-being; and ultimately believes that healing is possible. As you take steps toward healing and optimizing your relaxation response, these nine holistic habits will help guide you.

Consider your wholeness. You are the interconnection of your mind, body, and spirit, so as you take a holistic approach to healing your relaxation response and decreasing your stress, examine all of you, the whole person, not just one part or body system. Begin asking how your everyday life influences your ability to relax. How is your ability to relax influenced by the work you do, the relationships you're in, where and how you live, and the spaces where you spend time?

Consider the care that you're currently being provided and if it acknowledges and supports your wholeness. Does your care provider take all aspects of you and your life into consideration as you're being examined and as care plans are developed for your current state and future?

Signs and symptoms don't always tell the full story or explain why something is occurring, so it's important that as you work with care providers, they take the time to get to know you and ask exploratory questions. It's equally important that you give them as much information and detail as possible so you can work together toward solutions.

Pay attention. Your ability to pay attention, noticing what stress arises in your everyday life and what triggers it, can help you reverse the stress and its effects and increase your relaxation. Your willingness to be self-aware, in a nonjudgmental way, can open your eyes to insignificant stressors that have previously persisted that can now be addressed. Paying attention can also help you get closer to the root cause of your stress, as some things that need to be improved are simple fixes, while others will require some investigation and untangling to understand.

Paying attention will enable you to offer yourself grace and compassion as well. When you're unaware of why things are happening in your life, your internal criticism can be quite loud. Self-awareness can allow you to be a bit gentler and patient as you figure things out and do your best in the midst of learning how to rev up your relaxation response.

Trust the wisdom of your body. Your body is sending and receiving information all day long. It knows to alert you about hunger and thirst. It blinks, beats, and breathes without your consent. And it knows when you are exhausted and need to rest. Your body's job is to always keep you in a state of balance so that you can not only function but thrive.

The issues arise when you ignore that wisdom. When you refuse to drink water or get enough sleep. When you take on even more responsibility that causes you to feel stress and minimizes the amount of time you can spend cultivating meaningful relationships in your life. When you accept sedentary as your way of being because the culture offers extended periods of sitting as the new normal. It's often not the body that has failed. It is our failure to trust that the body knows exactly what you need to thrive, listening to that wisdom less and less as we experience life.

It's critical that you begin to believe in your own body first and foremost, before paying attention to any external influences. Your body truly wants to take care of you. So make it your mission to listen and learn what it's trying to tell you.

Begin with natural elements. Before trying invasive approaches that come with their own set of risks, start with natural elements.

Invasive approaches include the use of surgery or technology to address your pain, discomfort, or illness. Beginning with natural elements means ensuring that your nutritional intake is packed with a variety of nutrients from fruits, vegetables, herbs, spices, nuts, and water, which are the building blocks of the cells in your body and necessary for your body to heal on its own.

Starting natural also means moving your body in ways that can help release the toxins that can get stored in your cells, muscles, and fascia. If your body is harboring toxins, whether it be from the food you eat, the chemicals you come in contact with, emotional pain and trauma, or previous injury or illness, the toxins can cause you to experience even more pain and stress that's sometimes unexplainable, or invisible, but real and present.

When you begin with natural elements first, you give yourself the opportunity to notice how you feel and heal what could be a deficiency, allergy, overproduction, or lingering presence of something within your body. Without this step, you run the risk of having the problem recur or not actually healing anything.

Incorporate holistic practices and integrative care. Regularly incorporating holistic practices that induce the relaxation response, decrease stress, help you maintain your self-care, promote your health, and prevent illness can greatly improve your healing potential and ability to relax. The beauty of holistic practices is that they have a multitude of benefits that often overlap and build a supportive foundation for your overall well-being.

Holistic practices include prayer, meditation, aromatherapy, massage therapy, and a variety of other practices that we'll explore over the next several chapters. These practices are easily accessible and can generally be done anytime, from anywhere, with little to no cost and with undeniable benefits.

Integrative care coordinates the use of holistic practices and conventional medicine, often using the term *complementary practices* when referring to the intentional combination of the two.[1] When one uses holistic practices instead of, or as a replacement for, conventional medicine, practices are usually termed *alternative*.

Ask questions. Ask as many questions as possible of yourself, your care providers, and your community so that you can thoroughly understand what's taking place within and around you and find new ways to increase your relaxation. Ask yourself if the stress you're facing is a true threat and what you need to overcome it. Ask your care providers what resources are available that can enable you to decrease some of the stress in your life. Ask questions of your family and friends to determine what untapped resources are available to help support you as you strive to decrease your stress. Ask questions related to your education, finances, and relationships in order to provide yourself with as many tangible opportunities to rev up your relaxation response as possible.

Build a support system. Building a support system of family, friends, care providers, church, and community resources that understand your goals and will work with you in achieving them is vital to your success and the sustainability of rehabbing your relaxation response.

These trusted relationships remind you that you're not alone and offer the benefit of surrounding you with those you can rely on and confide in; they act as a buffer for the stress you're experiencing and open up space for deeper relaxation.

Believe. Probably the most important principle of all is the belief and expectation that healing is possible and will happen for you. You get to consciously choose your beliefs, including your ability to heal, relax, and reduce your stress. On the other hand, you can choose to believe that you'll never heal, that you'll become sicker, more stressed out, and die a premature death. The choice is always yours.

Yes, in the midst of modern advancements and technologies that can help cure sickness and disease, offer comfort, and provide care, you get to cultivate the belief that your body is good and designed to heal and regenerate, your mind is sound and set on the Spirit, and your spirit is in unison with Jehovah Rapha, the God who heals.

In previous years, the brain's ability to tap into its own healing powers when one believed a treatment would work was called the placebo effect. And currently, researchers are still trying to understand how a positive, life-affirming, expectant belief causes your brain to release feel-good hormones, endorphins, and medicating neurotransmitters that decrease pain, reduce stress, and at times put conditions into remission.

However, as a believer in Christ, your belief is not a result of a placebo, deception, or misinformation shared with you in an attempt to trick your brain into functioning a certain way or trusting false symbols and narratives as the source of your healing. Your belief is an active faith, conscious decision-making, and hope-fueled posture. Your belief doesn't require you to understand how healing will take place. Your belief is rooted in faith that even when you have no idea how healing will happen, or even what type of healing you need, you believe healing is an option and a possibility for you.

Your belief doesn't mean that you're solely relying on God to do the healing work for you, putting it in his hands and waiting for something to be done. Can this type of healing take place? Absolutely! Yet even though it can be done, this doesn't mean that you should passively sit by and disregard your responsibility. Quite the opposite. Be a proactive partner with God, creating an environment within and around you that supports natural and supernatural healing.

Create a plan. Creating a plan will give you a map for navigating this new territory of the relaxation response, helping you initiate and sustain the lifestyle changes necessary to make relaxation happen. Creating a plan will help you remain focused because you'll know exactly how to utilize your time and energy. It will also help you develop greater self-awareness and confidence as you begin to understand yourself, what it takes for you to follow through, and the realization that you're accomplishing your own goals.

The first step in creating your plan and making intentional changes is to set goals, and here's how you do that:

1. *Identify what you want to achieve.* This could be something specific like relaxing for five minutes each evening before bed or something more general like, "I want to relax my whole life."

2. *Make sure your goal is both realistic and achievable.* Consider your time, current resources, and abilities before setting your goal. You don't want to set yourself up for failure by aiming too high or too low.

3. *Write down your goal and make it specific.* Using the general goal from step one—"I want to relax my whole life"—here's an example of how to make a general goal specific by adding measurable details that you can track: "I want to intentionally relax after work for twenty minutes each day for the next two weeks."

4. *Break down your goal into smaller, manageable steps.* This will make it easier for you to track your progress and stay motivated.

5. *Set a deadline for achieving your goal.* For example, "I will begin my intentional relaxation practice this Sunday, and it will continue for the next two weeks." This will also help you stay focused and motivated to keep working toward your goal.

6. *Stay committed and hold yourself accountable.* Track your progress, celebrate your successes, and learn from any mistakes.

Setting goals is your first step, yet you'll still need to take action and work toward achieving your goal each day. Just remember that with persistence, prayer, patience, and perseverance, you can achieve anything you set your mind to.

As you respond holistically, understand that you can't fail at relaxing. Every effort to relax is beneficial and engages your relaxation response, so take it one step at a time and use the practices in the following chapters to support your efforts.

RELEASE

Which aspects of yourself, your life, and your wholeness have you ignored or been neglecting? How is this causing you stress?

Is there an area of your life that you feel disconnected from or uninterested in? Can you identify the reason you feel this way so you can gradually begin restoring the connection?

REESTABLISH

When Jesus saw him lie, and knew that he had been now a long time in that case, he saith unto him, Wilt thou be made whole? (John 5:6 KJV)

GOD made my life complete when I placed all the pieces before him. When I got my act together, he gave me a fresh start. Now I'm alert to GOD's ways; I don't take GOD for granted. Every day I review the ways he works; I try not to miss a trick. I feel put back together, and I'm watching my step. GOD rewrote the text of my life when I opened the book of my heart to his eyes. (Psalm 18:20-24 MSG)

RECEIVE

How to practice journaling for relaxation. A practice that requires few resources or expertise, journaling offers you the space to reflect, reveal, and release whatever you're harboring, and heal whatever is hurting.

I've witnessed those who've experienced traumatic events and were left speechless. And others, in an effort to keep everything in them from falling apart, simply refuse to allow words to depart from their lips.

In these moments of heartache and despair, being handed a pen often feels safer and doable, giving you a simple tool to begin clearing your mind and mending your wounds.

As both an art form and a healing practice, journaling effectively offers you the space to reflect upon and capture life's memorable moments and let go of painful experiences and broken identities.

As believers, we must do the often-challenging work of surrendering our pain instead of suppressing or suffering from it, expressing and exercising our faith to create space to be fully healed.

A practice that only requires you to be honest and vulnerable with yourself, journaling can help you work toward the root cause of what you're experiencing and why, breaking open the pathway to your healing and transformation, and beckoning greater relaxation.

Some of the immediate therapeutic benefits of journaling include alleviation of stress, improved immune function, boosted spiritual connection, lowered blood pressure, enhanced mental focus, and faster, more thorough healing.

So simply begin to write. Journal what currently is, and the vision for the healing you desire to take place.

From this space of honesty with self and God, continue to release your heart's desires, resting in the wholeness and healing your relationship with him has made available to you.

Whether the wounds that need your attention are deep or superficial, journaling is a balm, helping you soothe and sort through what's present and position you for the future.

You can allow the Lord to use the gift of journaling to break what has bound you, to mend what's currently broken, to breathe life into dying situations, and to bring love, light, and joy into dark and discouraging situations. In his presence and in the words on the page, you'll experience the relaxation you're in need of.

To engage your relaxation response through the practice of journaling, begin by setting a timer for five to ten minutes. Choose a topic or a journal prompt, or allow whatever is on your mind to guide the words you write on the page. Continue writing until your timer goes off, or until you feel a shift in your mind and body. This shift may be a sense of calm as the relaxation response is activated, or you may experience a flood of emotions as your feelings are released through journaling. With consistent practice, you'll be able to face whatever it is you're experiencing and intentionally elicit your relaxation response.

How to use sound for relaxation. Sound is a form of energy made by vibrations. A sound wave radiates from its source, generated by the movement of energy traveling through something, such as air, water, or any other solid, liquid, or gas. The vibration from the source bumps into the molecules close to them, causing them to vibrate as well. This wave of movement carries the sound energy in all directions, decreasing in intensity the farther it travels from the source.

Because the molecules in our bodies vibrate, sound is not only heard, but experienced through every cell. This also makes sound healing and therapies possible.

Sound therapy is a practice that uses sound, music, and instruments in therapeutic ways to enhance the healing and well-being of the listener. It's often combined with deep self-reflection techniques to support the mind, body, and spirit, and decreases stress, promotes relaxation, and improves overall health.

There are multiple ways to practice sound therapy. Listening to relaxing music is a simple and therapeutic way to experience the benefits of sound. I enjoy listening to natural sounds such as waterfalls, thunderstorms, and ocean waves, yet there are so many options to choose from. The key is to keep searching for the sounds that bring you the deepest sense of relaxation.

Another way to practice sound therapy is through sound baths, an immersive and therapeutic listening experience that uses sound to relax and restore mind, body, spirit healing and harmony. This practice can be one-on-one or in a group setting, and uses instruments such as singing bowls, chimes, harps, didgeridoos, gongs, and the human voice.

A sound bath session can take anywhere from twenty minutes to two hours with various beneficial effects experienced throughout, such as waves of emotional release and the deep sense of relaxation.

Hearing the Word of God. After waking, some previously comatose patients describe being able to hear what was going on around them, even if they couldn't respond. This is because auditory stimuli and sound are still being captured by the brain. This is important so that you understand the significance of speaking and listening to the Word of God.

Speaking the Word of God creates an audible sound that we are then able to hear. And hearing the Word of God has transformative power, whether or not one is yet conscious or responsive to it. As we're told in Romans 10:17, "Consequently, faith comes from hearing the message, and the message is heard through the word about Christ."

So hearing the Word of God, either through personally speaking the Scriptures or actively listening to them, increases your faith, changes your condition, and can shift you out of a stressful state of being.

We also find in Scripture that God wants to hear the sound of our praise. Psalm 150:6 tells us, "Let everything that has breath praise the Lord. Praise the Lord." And Hebrews 13:15 goes on to say, "Through Jesus, therefore, let us continually offer to God a sacrifice of praise— the fruit of lips that openly profess his name." How deeply we can relax knowing that the sound of our sacrificial praise is pleasing to God and honors him.

How to use aromatherapy for relaxation. Two of the first treasures offered to Jesus when he was born were frankincense and myrrh, aromatic substances used in spiritual ceremonies and heavenly worship. Throughout the Bible we find references to aromatic botanicals, fragrant offerings, and aromas that were pleasing to the Lord. Genesis 1:11 says, "Then God said, 'Let the land produce vegetation: seed-bearing plants and trees on the land that bear fruit with seed in it, according to their various kinds.' And it was so." This verse illustrates that God made provision when he created the earth to allow it to bear all types of plants that would support our existence and could be used in a variety of ways.

Today, we describe aromatherapy as a holistic healing treatment that uses natural plant extracts to relax and soothe the body, mind, and spirit and promote health and well-being. It can be used to reduce stress and anxiety, improve sleep, boost energy levels, and improve moods. Aromatherapy uses essential oils, highly concentrated plant extracts from the leaves, roots, bark, stem, and seeds, to provide therapeutic benefits. These oils can be used in a variety of ways, such as through topical application, massage, inhalation, or diffusing into the air. Essential oils that promote relaxation include, but are not limited to, lavender, bergamot, roman chamomile, ylang-ylang, and sandalwood.

Create an essential oil blend. To create an aromatherapy blend for relaxation, you could combine lavender, chamomile, and sandalwood essential oils. Lavender has a calming and soothing scent that helps reduce stress and anxiety. Chamomile is calming, helps to reduce inflammation, and is known for its antianxiety and sedative properties. Sandalwood has a sweet and woody aroma that helps to promote relaxation and peacefulness.

When combining these oils, I suggest using a few drops of lavender, two drops of chamomile, and one drop of sandalwood. You can add the oils to a diffuser or bath for a calming, relaxing aromatherapy experience.

Additional ways to practice aromatherapy. Add five drops of lavender essential oil to a diffuser to inhale the relaxing benefits. Add chamomile leaves and several drops of chamomile essential oil to a warm bath. Add ylang-ylang essential oil to a carrier oil for a soothing massage.

If you don't have essential oils but want to give aromatherapy a try, you can combine ingredients on your stovetop to produce a relaxing effect. Combine the peel of an orange, several sprigs of rosemary, and ginger (ground or a half-inch-thick slice) in a pot of simmering water. The essential oils will seep out and fill the air with a calming scent. Another stovetop aromatherapy blend uses the peel of a lime and fresh basil and mint leaves.

Things to know about aromatherapy. A carrier oil such as coconut, jojoba, avocado, or grapeseed oil is used to dilute essential oils before they are applied to the skin in massage and aromatherapy.

You should always complete a patch test on a small area of skin before applying an essential oil to a larger area of your body. So before you add them to your bath, use them during massage, or apply them to large areas of skin, test out how your body reacts to the essential oil within a small area to determine if you'll have an allergic reaction. To complete a patch test, mix a drop or two of the essential oil you desire to test into a carrier oil and apply to a small patch of skin on the inside of your arm. The area should be no larger than a large coin. If you do develop a reaction, such as red, itchy, or swollen skin, wash off the area as soon as possible. If you do not develop a reaction, you can proceed using the tested essential oil and carrier oil with caution. Avoid applying essential oils to broken skin, near your eyes, and to other sensitive areas.

It's important to note that some essential oils have photosensitive properties and may cause skin irritation if exposed to direct sunlight after use. Some of these essential oils include citrus oils such as bergamot, lemon, lime, orange, and grapefruit.

If you are pregnant, it's important to be aware that some essential oils can cause uterine contractions, and others should be avoided completely while pregnant.

As with every practice, make sure you're consulting with your care provider before use.

PRAYER

Lord, you desire our wholeness, that we return to you for restoration of broken relationship and heart. Thank you for mending the pieces of our lives and stories, for creating us anew. We are whole and in your hands, and for that we are thankful. In Jesus' name, amen.

6

Resuscitate Your Power

WE KNEW IT WAS TIME to wake up our older children and leave for the hospital. But when my husband returned from loading our sleepy children into the van, I couldn't move.

"Should I call 911?" he asked as calmly as he could. I felt like I was watching my own movie unfold. After laboring for a couple of hours and clocking what I thought were impossibly close contractions coming one right after another, I was keenly aware that we would never make it. It was time. I *knew* the baby was coming.

I never thought she'd enter the world as quickly as she did, but there she was. The commotion scared the children, who then came running back into the house to meet their new baby sister.

I did it, I thought. *I really did it.*

I'd given birth to all of our children without any form of medication, but it was always in a hospital.

I've always felt most powerful in the minutes and weeks after giving birth. Embracing the beauty and sheer wonder of my body—what it's capable of is nothing short of miraculous.

But this time, there I stood, responding to the needs of my body and my baby, without protocol, policy, or standard procedure standing in my way.

That was different. *That* was powerful.

This time unveiled another level of possibility and made evident a few problems as well.

I was left wondering:

What else am I capable of that the world, or our culture, tells me I'm unqualified, incompetent, or in need of support in order to accomplish?

How many unnecessary interventions are women subjected to because they're not allowed to follow their instincts or because labor and birth have become medical procedures instead of a natural process?

Why, after finding out that I gave birth at home, did so many people share their fear-based perspectives, instead of simply affirming what just took place?

Some of the common sentiments were: *You must have been so scared. Thank God you're all right. I'm so glad nothing went wrong.*

Not for a minute did I feel afraid of what was happening, nor did I expect any complications. And yes, I'm glad there were none. But how exactly did we get here? After reflection on my experience, I've learned a few things.

First, labor and birth are viewed as medical procedures that need to take place under medical supervision in order to be done "right" or well. This view, however, undermines a woman's ability to labor and give birth, and suggests that someone other than you knows what's best for you and your baby.

No matter what type of procedure, intervention, or care you're in need of, you need to make wise, informed, fear-free decisions, and trust the wisdom of your body. To the best of your ability, know what you're doing and why you're doing it. Ask questions. Know your options—the pros, the cons, and the side effects. Participate in your health and well-being. Be your own biggest advocate. Never voluntarily hand over your power. Don't be a victim of bullying. And refuse to allow fear to play a part in your decision-making.

Second, I've also noticed that many have become afraid of their own bodies, either inheriting or becoming indoctrinated with myths and fears about the bodies they inhabit. When this is the case, you have to unlearn what you believe so that you can learn to trust the wisdom of your body. Doing so takes time and practice, and it helps you develop a level of confidence in your body that'll keep you from relying on and handing over responsibility to others for your health and healing.

When you take the time to truly listen and respond to what it seems your body is asking you for, you won't need as many second opinions. You begin to navigate using your own discernment about what you do and don't need to maintain your well-being.

The third and final thing I learned from this experience is that I'm as amazingly powerful as I thought I was, and yet I'm still influenced by the thoughts and fears of others.

I did it. I gave birth at home to our beautiful, healthy baby girl. But birthing at home or in a birthing center was something that I always believed I could do. I simply wouldn't do it because it made other people too uncomfortable.

It wasn't traditional or the norm and seemed to bring up more questions and concerns than I thought were worth debating. But as I now see to an even greater extent, doing unconventional things that help shift and reshape the perspective of others is woven into my story.[1]

This experience helped me access power I wasn't aware I could embody, and it helped me see that no matter what aspect of my life it may be, I'm under no obligation to make my decisions make sense to others. And *that* is equally as powerful.

TAKE CHARGE OF YOUR HEALTH

Making choices and implementing practices that improve your health over time mean that you're taking charge of your health. One of the actions you can take involves choosing the right health care provider for your current and future health and lifestyle goals.

When it comes to your care providers, take whatever time is necessary to do your research and determine who you enjoy being around, trust, and feel comfortable with. This partnership influences your health and future, and if rushed into, could cause you more pain and frustration than necessary.

Think of the process as if you're interviewing a new member of your own personal care team. Schedule office visits to meet potential care providers and determine whether or not you're a good fit. If you're unable to do this, check their website to learn more about them, and search for online reviews to read the perspectives of their patients and clients.

If you're able to engage with them, either in person or online, before officially becoming a patient or client, ask questions so you can learn how their practice works. Your relationship with your care provider is crucial to your health and healing, so do yourself a favor and partner with those who truly support you in reaching your wellness goals.

After choosing your provider, it's your job to show up prepared with details about what you're going through and your personal health and wellness goals. Visiting your health care provider should look like a partnership with you leading the way. You shouldn't hand over your existence or healing ability to someone who may be meeting you for the first time, or who's only getting a snapshot of your total being. And just in case you are unaware of this, your participation means that you get to say no, get second opinions, check side effects, thoroughly read through consent forms, and ask as many questions as you need to.

As a health care consumer, you must make many decisions about the care you receive. Who should my health care provider be? What hospital should I visit in an emergency? Is this insurance plan right for me and my family? And so on.

As decisions are being made, it's your responsibility to make wise choices, to be well informed and actively participate in your health and care. Begin by figuring out your options.

Utilize your options. Remember when you searched for those shoes online for an hour? You should put just as much effort into searching for your health care providers. Although your insurance provider may guide you to the care providers within your network, you are free to visit, consult with, and pay any care provider you wish to help you reach your health and wellness goals. You can search for providers online, get referrals from friends and family, or ask your insurance provider to give you a list of available practitioners based on your needs.

Pay attention to the values and beliefs of the care providers you're researching. Ask yourself if they are in alignment with who you are mentally, spiritually, emotionally, and physically, and if they offer the types of services you're looking for.

Understand informed consent. Informed consent is an autonomous decision made by a person after having been provided with the relevant facts and risks of a medical intervention. This includes the option to accept, delay, or decline any test, procedure, or medicine.

All medical professionals are required to obtain consent for procedures. Consent cannot be coerced and should only include the facts about your procedure or drug, including, but not limited to, the side effects.

Ask questions. You have the right to ask questions before consenting to any test, procedure, or medication. If you don't understand what is taking place, ask questions. Your practitioner should be forthcoming with information and resources and should take your unique needs and situation into consideration. You should continue to ask questions until you are confident that you have the information necessary to make an informed decision.

Advocate. You are your best advocate. Asking questions of your health care providers and taking charge of your health may seem like a bold act, but it will ensure that you're fully informed and aware of what is taking place in and to your body. Decisions that are aligned with your values and desires may fall outside of the realm of standard practice, and may even be viewed as an inconvenience, but it is your right to decide.

Don't be bullied into a decision because you have not taken the time to ask questions or learn about your rights, or because you are afraid to stand up for yourself. Being informed is another way to care for your mind, body, and spirit and ensure that you're receiving holistic care. The more you take charge of your health, the more confident and empowered you'll feel about making decisions that are best for your health and well-being.

Prevent. I initially learned about many of the integrative practices I share throughout this book because they were being used in the treatment or recovery of patients who'd already experienced sickness and surgery.

Even before some of these practices became trendy or mainstream, I thought, *If these practices are good enough to help heal and nurture people back to health and wellness, shouldn't we be using them to sustain wellness and prevent sicknesses before they ever occur?* Integrative practices that reduce stress, support wellness, and promote relaxation are essential elements in any preventive care plan. And prevention of disease is always better, and easier, than an attempt to cure disease.

Preventive care promotes healthy lifestyles, offers education and resources, provides early treatment for illnesses, and prioritizes foundational health practices such as nutrition, sleep, and exercise. Visiting a care provider for wellness checks, getting health screenings, and receiving health counseling are also preventive measures that significantly reduce the risk of disease, disability, or death.

Listen to your intuition. Intuition is something that you know instinctively, outside of conscious reasoning. Often it's the gut feeling that you have. The internal alert system that has little tangible evidence and may even be difficult to explain. Yet you just know.

Your intuition can tell you when something is off in your body. It can help you sense danger in the world around you. Or make you think twice when a care provider suggests something that you should or shouldn't do regarding your health.

Issues usually happen when you stop listening to or start second-guessing your intuition. When you put more faith in external information and influences than you do in yourself. Now, of course I'm not telling you to ignore the trusted provider that you partnered with for your care. However, I am telling you not to ignore your intuition.

Your intuition offers you guidance, and it doesn't always make any sense to those around you. So if you find yourself in a situation that seems too hard to explain or that others you are interacting with can't seem to understand, give yourself the time and space you need to process what's taking place.

Listening to your intuition will require you to speak up for yourself because you have insight or a perspective that no one else does. Doing so might take some practice, but when it comes to your health and well-being, it is absolutely worth it.

Don't allow someone's job title or profession or society's perspective of the role they play in the world stop you from listening to your own intuition or minimize it. It is more powerful than most even realize and can help you make decisions that are best for you, your health, and your healing.

Stop seeking balance. Balance is overrated and unattainable. There is no way that I can give equal parts of my time and attention to every facet of my life. However, I can be present with what's right in front of me, striving for harmony and a pleasant combination of the many parts of my life. Striving for balance, on the other hand, will leave you feeling inadequate and unable to ever reach your goals. You'll feel at war with yourself instead of being able to embrace the beautiful options available to you. Just remember that harmony happens within you before it happens around you. Center yourself and let harmony be your guide.

Know your medicine. In order to safely and effectively make informed decisions about your health and healing, it's important to understand that there are various types of medicines and medical practices. Knowing your medicine and why you're choosing it is a powerful way to keep yourself safe, optimize your healing, and increase your ability to relax.

Ayurvedic medicine, an ancient healing system from India, is a holistic approach designed to help restore natural equilibrium and promote overall health. It focuses on the physical, mental, and spiritual aspects of well-being, utilizing herbs and lifestyle changes to bring the body back into balance.

Botanical medicine uses plants and plant substances, taken orally or applied topically, to treat a variety of medical conditions. It has been used for centuries to promote health and healing, as well as prevent and treat disease. Botanical medicine's natural ingredients are gentle on the body, treat multiple conditions at once, and potentially cause fewer side effects than traditional pharmaceuticals.

Chiropractic medicine is a form of complementary medicine that focuses on the diagnosis, treatment, and prevention of mechanical disorders of the musculoskeletal system. It's a hands-on approach to care that uses physical manipulation, mobilization, and other manual techniques to help improve range of motion, posture, and overall balance.

Homeopathy uses small doses of natural substances to stimulate the body's innate healing abilities. The practice is based on the principle of "like cures like," using a substance that can cause certain symptoms in a healthy person to treat those same symptoms in a sick person.

Naturopathy aims to restore the body's natural balance to help it heal itself. It uses nontoxic, natural therapies such as herbal remedies, massage, nutrition, exercise, and lifestyle changes to treat illness.

Osteopathic medicine focuses on the whole body and its structures, working to provide preventive care and healing through manual manipulation of the bones, muscles, joints, and soft tissues in the body.

Traditional Chinese medicine (TCM) has been used in China for thousands of years and is based on the belief that health and well-being depend on the balance between opposing forces, yin and yang, as well as the flow of *qi* (vital energy). TCM uses various techniques such as herbal medicine, acupuncture, massage, and dietary therapy.

Many of these practices can be used alone or in conjunction with conventional medicine. When considering any medicine or medical practice, speak with an experienced professional about your goals, and remember that you can always change your mind about the care you're participating in and wish to receive.

Connect to power. Hospitals have backup generators so that if the power goes out, crucial, life-sustaining equipment doesn't shut off, harming patients and disconnecting them from the care they need. But this only works if the machines are plugged into the proper outlet.

You see, although there are outlets all around the hospital room, not every outlet is connected to the generator. This means that not every outlet supplies the same power or ability to back you up or sustain you in an emergency.

As a holistic nurse, I can give you all types of information, resources, and practices that will support your healing and relaxation, but ultimately, if you aren't plugged into God, the One who sustains you, supplies your power, and backs you up whenever you need him to, none of these practices will save you. You must take responsibility for your own care, fixing the things that are well within your control, and making a habit out of caring for the vessel God has given you.

Let's Relax

RELEASE

What have you been unwilling to face or address in your life even though it's causing you stress?

In what ways have you yielded your power to others, and how has that caused you stress?

REESTABLISH

For the Spirit God gave us does not make us timid, but gives us power, love and self-discipline. (2 Timothy 1:7)

For the kingdom of God is not a matter of talk but of power. (1 Corinthians 4:20)

RECEIVE

How to practice self-compassion for relaxation. Following a reconciled relationship with God, the most significant relationship you can seek to restore is the one with yourself. Learning to love yourself, forgive yourself, and offer yourself compassion will extend to all the other relationships you participate in.

Colossians 3:12 says, "Therefore, as God's chosen people, holy and dearly loved, clothe yourselves with compassion, kindness, humility, gentleness and patience." The directive of this verse extends outwardly, toward our neighbors, and it also applies to the way we treat ourselves. Self-compassion is directed inward, toward oneself, treating yourself with the same level of concern and kindness you'd show to a friend who was struggling. Self-compassion is a consciousness of your own distress, and the desire to alleviate it. It's understanding that you're not alone in your mistakes and weaknesses. It acknowledges that failures are a part of normal everyday life for everyone and welcomes you into this commonality of humanity.

Self-compassion is understanding that you are deserving of care just like everyone else and enables you to treat yourself with the kindness you'd offer a dear friend. Self-compassion helps you become mindful of your feelings and emotions, creates space for you to remain calm when you're faced with criticism, failure, and rejection, and is a source of empowerment and inner strength that involves facing failure, insecurities, and mistakes in a productive way.

Some of the benefits of self-compassion are an increase in overall well-being, a boost in feelings of self-worth and resilience, improved body image, higher emotional intelligence, increased motivation to improve on mistakes, greater overall satisfaction in life, and decreases in anxiety, depression, and fear of failure. And the good thing is, self-compassion can be learned. So let's practice.

Think about an area in your life where you've been suffering from stress. What would you say to a child or your best friend if they shared that same struggle with you? Now take the same words you would speak and the empathy that you'd feel toward them, and offer it toward yourself. This is an act of self-compassion.

Acknowledging your self-criticism is an act of self-compassion. And after you acknowledge it, forgive yourself. I don't know about you, but occasionally I can be hard on myself. My desire is for the information that I share with you in this book to be more than my knowledge. I want it to be an example of how I live my life. The reality is, there are moments when I'm stretched thin and days when I don't stop to check in with myself. But instead of wasting time beating myself up about it, I forgive myself for existing in a way that's out of alignment with who I want to be, extending myself the same compassion I would toward others.

Releasing unmet expectations and timelines of what you thought would happen in your life is another way to show yourself compassion. It can be heavy and unnecessarily burdensome to hold on to any pain or disappointment based on fantasized visions of what you desired your life to look like. This includes any expectations you have for others to behave in a certain way, or to create for you what you're envisioning, understanding that you already have a Savior, and that is not their role. Praying and releasing those desires and disappointments over to God can help you see your way forward according to the plans God has for you, and help you appreciate what is and what is to come.

How to use deep listening for relaxation. The Bible teaches us that listening to instruction is a skill that cultivates our faith (Romans 10:17), wisdom (Proverbs 19:20), security, and ease (Proverbs 1:33). And we know that as we listen to God for instruction and communion, we also want him to listen to us whenever we cry out to him. One of the ways to continuously develop our listening skills is to utilize the practice of deep listening, which is another act of self-compassion that'll help you reestablish your relationship and connection with yourself. It's the act of pausing to check in and hear your own needs, struggles, and desires.

When you practice deep listening, you can better see and feel what's going on in your mind and body. You can hear your body without judgment, in a state of ease, because of the safe and inviting space that you're creating.

Deep listening is critical to our ability to heal the areas in which we've learned to mistrust ourselves. When we allow our work, and the world, to tell us to keep going and to do more, as we shove down our own desire for rest, shame ourselves for needing a break, or silence ourselves so we dare not miss an alarm, a call, a cry, or any other sign that others are in trouble or in need of our help, we tune out our instincts and become our own neglectful enemy.

I wholeheartedly believe that you already know what you need. Because you are constantly talking to you. Deep listening is what makes you aware of the conversation.

Psalm 37:4 reminds us that when you are a believer and you delight yourself in the Lord, he will give you the desires of your heart, and you will come to understand that he is the answer to all of your longings. Spending time listening, praying, journaling, and meditating creates space for God to reveal his will to you and for you to hear it.

One of my favorite ways to deeply listen to myself is to get outside and go for a walk among the trees or along the water. All types of things rise to the surface, including godly insight, when I allow myself to listen and be fully present with me.

How to play for relaxation. Proverbs 17:22 reminds us, "A cheerful heart is good medicine, but a crushed spirit dries up the bones." This verse expresses the importance of actually enjoying your life, having something to look forward to, and spending at least some of your time being playful. Doing so cultivates joy, makes meaningful memories, helps you release any stress and tension that may be building up in your life, and relaxes you.

Not only can play boost your mood, energy, clarity, and joy, it can enhance your relationships and make work more enjoyable. And the joy you experience through play is critical to your well-being.

When you play, your body releases your feel-good hormones, helping you heal and restore balance internally. It also gives your mind and spirit a chance to relax and stay in alignment with what truly matters in your life, versus becoming stuck in meaningless activity or continuing to hold on to stressors.

Playing can look very different for you based on what you enjoy, where you live, and the time you set aside for it. So never allow the world to tell you you're too anything to play. You're not too old, too busy, too professional, too responsible, too far into parenthood, too Christian, too whatever. Do what you enjoy as often as you can, and you'll begin to experience deeper relaxation and greater well-being.

Take the time to remember what you enjoy doing, everything from childhood games and travel to sports events and arts and crafts. Then plan to routinely incorporate play into your life. You can try new things and play as often as you want or need to. Just remember that overindulging may lead to neutral feelings about your activities of choice, so pace yourself!

Try one of these ways to play:

- color
- take a road trip
- dance
- have a party
- sing
- take a class in art, music, poetry, or yoga
- plan a girls' night out
- ride a bike
- go to a comedy show
- run on the beach
- go camping
- attend a concert
- go to a spa
- read a book
- play a board game
- go to an arcade
- take a vacation
- visit an amusement park
- go to a sporting event
- watch a movie

- play with your children
- play with a pet
- make or build something with your hands

How to use creativity for relaxation. I believe we're all artists with the ability to create, and no matter which mediums we choose, creativity allows us to offer something meaningful and inspiring to the rest of the world while we offer ourselves therapeutic space to heal, reflect, and co-create with God.

Art therapy. Our brains and bodies transform as we experience art. Whether we're creating or encountering art, the reward center of our brain is activated, we're able to envision a more hopeful future, and our cortisol levels lower significantly.

Art therapy can help one communicate thoughts and feelings that are difficult to put into words, make sense of things, relax in the face of difficult situations, improve self-esteem, develop self-awareness, and provide a chance to connect with others in a safe, nonjudgmental way.

Art therapy can include drawing, sculpting, painting, coloring, writing, photography, collage, and pottery, among other options.

Dance therapy. This is based on the idea that the mind, body, and spirit are interconnected and inseparable, therefore movement can be therapeutic and promote physical, mental, emotional, and spiritual health and well-being.

Dance and movement develop more effective communication and relationship skills, creating new coping mechanisms while improving self-esteem and body image.

Music therapy. This therapy uses relaxing or comforting music to impact and improve health and well-being. Music therapy has the ability to reduce stress, improve mood, and help one express oneself. Music therapy includes singing, playing instruments, listening to music, and discussing the meaning of lyrics.

Although music therapy can be practiced with a music therapist, you can practice therapeutic techniques at any time.

Other creative therapies include writing, gardening, and even cooking. Experiment with different creative activities to find those you enjoy and can make a part of your relaxation routine.

PRAYER

Omnipotent God, time and time again you have bestowed a spirit of power upon us. Guide us to navigate this life assured that we are powerful beyond measure, and in those moments when we are weak and weary, to trust that we can depend on the strength and power you will provide. Help us never to fear the fullness of power available to us, so that we can use it to your glory. In Jesus' name, amen.

7

Review Your Surroundings

EACH PATIENT WHO ENTERS THE HOSPITAL HAS A STORY. Unfortunately, most of that story remains a mystery because of time constraints that prevent in-depth conversations with each person in need of care. But often, what we don't see or talk about has an equally significant impact on health, the ability to heal, and the stress being experienced.

The places we live, work, and play, including the conditions of those spaces, directly affect how we exist. So let's examine the stress within our surroundings.

ENVIRONMENTAL STRESS

Environmental stress is caused by natural or anthropogenic elements, meaning that it results from human actions, in one's surroundings or environment, producing mental, physical, spiritual, or emotional stress.

Our environment includes the air we breathe, the food we eat, the water we drink, the places where we live and work, and the natural world around us, and when the environment is polluted, it can lead to all sorts of health problems.

Environments with cluttered spaces can greatly contribute to the stress one experiences. Clutter is a collection of things that take up space in a poorly organized way. The presence of clutter can activate the stress response as it signals to our brains that our work is not, and may never be, done. It decreases productivity as it bombards our minds with excessive stimuli, which causes our senses to work overtime.

Clutter can drain you of positive energy and make you feel anxious, depressed, angry, and overwhelmed.

Noise has a similarly stressful impact as clutter. Noise, or sound pollution, involves harmful, excessive, unwanted, or disturbing sounds that affect one's health and well-being and stimulates the stress response. Noise pollution has been linked with cardiovascular disease, increased blood pressure, oxidative stress, aggression, disrupted sleep patterns, headaches, hearing loss, and impaired learning. According to the World Health Organization (WHO), the weekly average noise exposure from leisure sources such as personal listening devices should be less than 80dB, and the yearly noise exposure average is recommended to be less than 70dB.[1]

Unfortunately, the air we breathe isn't always a high-quality, life-sustaining element. The air we breathe can greatly contribute to the stress we experience. For example, poor air quality can lead to respiratory diseases, oxidative stress, and inflammation, laying a foundation for chronic diseases. Poor air quality can also be responsible for asthma attacks, eye, nose, and throat irritation, heart attacks, and premature deaths. It can also cause neurological and cognitive changes. Air pollutants include dust, dirt, soot, smoke, ozone, carbon monoxide, airborne lead, radon, methane, exhaust, gasoline vapors, and chemical solvents. Low concentrations of ozone can trigger lung irritation and inflammation, coughing, wheezing, and asthma attacks or increase one's susceptibility to respiratory illnesses. Particulate pollution can cause bronchitis, coughing, asthma attacks, decreased lung function, painful breathing, and cardiac problems. Air pollution makes exercise and outdoor work more difficult and can contribute to further inflammation and disease. When air quality is poor or air quality alerts are active, you should limit your time outside to avoid hazardous conditions.

And let's not forget to discuss radiation. Waves of radiation can come from the sun, cell phones, computers, medical or dental use of X-rays, or from radon, which can seep up from the soil and into your home. Radiation can damage the DNA in our cells, and in high doses can result in nausea and vomiting, hair loss, acute radiation syndrome, skin redness, radiation burns, or even death.

Water, the most abundant natural resource on the planet, once contaminated, can become difficult to fix. Water stress occurs when the demand for safe, usable water in a given area exceeds the supply. Contaminants such as plastics, heavy metals, radiation, sewage, microorganisms, and agricultural chemical runoff pollute water systems and make water unsafe for consumption, and chemical or oil spills can permanently taint a water source. Forever chemicals, which never break down, are used in food wrappers, firefighting foam, sunscreens, and other products where plastic is altered to be heat resistant and more durable; these chemicals can now be found in almost half the tap water in the United States.

Other elements in our climate can heighten our stress. Extreme weather, melting ice, rising waters, forest fires, and excessive heat all increase the likelihood of illness and negative health outcomes, including heat associated illnesses, water-borne and vector-borne diseases, and respiratory illnesses.

TOXINS AND CHEMICALS

Exposure to toxins such as asbestos, lead, mold, and mildew stresses the body and causes disease. Pesticides have known carcinogenic factors, and dioxin, a highly toxic byproduct of manufacturing processes, is a serious and persistent environmental pollutant that can lead to heart disease, cancer, and type 2 diabetes.

Environmental hormone disruptors, also known as endocrine disruptors, are thought to disrupt normal endocrine function even with very low exposure levels. Endocrine-disrupting chemicals are synthetic, or manmade, chemicals that can mimic, interfere with, or block how your hormones function within your body. Some of the well-studied disrupters include bisphenols, including bisphenol A (BPA), polychlorinated biphenyls (PCBs), phthalates, dichlorodiphenyltrichloroethane (DDT), and dichlorodiphenyldichloroethylene (DDE).

These endocrine disruptors are found in everyday products including food and beverage packaging, some cosmetics, toys, carpet, and pesticides. Endocrine disruptors affect male and female reproduction, metabolism, obesity, breast development and cancer, prostate cancer, and cardiovascular endocrinology, the endocrine mechanism the heart uses to communicate with the rest of the body.[2]

STRESS AND VIOLENCE

Chronic exposure to violence is a stressor that can lead to increased stress reactivity, asthma exacerbations, increased aggression, and disruptions in emotion regulation processes. Stress may also influence an increase in violent behavior, causing one to become verbally or physically aggressive and lose control more frequently.

Stress is cumulative, building over time, so the number of environmental stressors that one encounters, including noise, crowding, exposure to violence, and temperature—consider the rise in crime during the warmer months of the year—increase the likelihood that stress is expressed as violent behavior.

SHIFTING YOUR SURROUNDINGS

A person's zip code influences overall health outcomes, the level of stress they experience, and their life expectancy.[3] Where we live often contributes to social factors like unemployment or excessive working hours in an attempt to make ends meet, access to health insurance, cultural influences on behaviors, and coping mechanisms such as alcohol, smoking, drugs, poor nutrition, and unhealthy physical activity.

Thankfully, our surroundings can be changed. As we begin to examine what we're surrounded by and become intentional about shifting away from stressful surroundings, we create space to experience healing and to become less-stressed versions of ourselves. When packing up and moving isn't an option, we can cultivate less stressful environments within our home and community that can act as spaces of refuge in the midst of stressful external circumstances beyond our control.

God originally placed humankind in an earthly paradise, the Garden of Eden. A space that he planted with what was desirable and pleasing to the sight and good for food, and he ensured that rivers flowed to water the garden (Genesis 2:9). The thoughtfulness and intention to provide an environment that offered everything needed for his creation to grow, thrive, and experience beauty demonstrates God's care for such spaces and the potential they have to heal, nurture, and relax us.

NURSING'S ENVIRONMENTAL THEORY

It was a nurse, Florence Nightingale, who made the correlation of clean water, fresh air, light, cleanliness, and sanitation with a patient's health outcomes, demonstrating that a healthy physical environment is essential for healing. This discovery led to nursing's environmental theory, in which the nursing profession intentionally utilizes the patient's environment to assist in recovery, facilitate healing, promote relaxation, and optimize well-being.

Even with the intention nurses and hospitals place on the environment's ability to nurture someone's health, I believe spas are the ultimate blueprint for healing spaces. Of course, one who goes to a spa is unlikely to be terribly ill or in need of the equipment and resources hospitals provide, but there is wisdom to be gleaned from the intention behind spa design.

Spas are in the hospitality business and take a holistic approach to well-being, offering spaces that nurture and delight the senses, promote a healing lifestyle, and relax your mind, body, and spirit. Their intentional biophilic design connects visitors to the natural environment whether they're indoors or out, with circadian lighting, calming colors, nourishing treatments, and boundless depths of relaxing spaces and experiences that allow stress to melt away.

And although I'm always available for a spa getaway, wouldn't it be amazing to create a space of your own so you wouldn't have to escape your own life to experience retreat?

Let's Relax

RELEASE

Which spaces in your life stress and deplete you?

Where is there physical clutter that is negatively impacting you that can be tended to?

REESTABLISH

> The heavens declare the glory of God; the skies proclaim the work of his hands. (Psalm 19:1)

> For since the creation of the world God's invisible qualities—his eternal power and divine nature—have been clearly seen, being understood from what has been made, so that people are without excuse. (Romans 1:20)

RECEIVE

How to create a healing environment. Ecclesiastes 3:11 says, "He has made everything beautiful in its time. He has also set eternity in the human heart." So as long as we live, time cannot bring fulfillment, and we will long for the experience of eternity, including the beauty of our heavenly home. Until eternity is realized, we can try to create a sense of beauty and harmony within our temporary, earthly dwelling places in the form of healing environments.

A healing environment fosters a nurturing, therapeutic effect that can help reduce stress and anxiety, evoke feelings of serenity and calm, lessen pain, and promote a sense of well-being. You can create your healing environment anywhere.[4]

Begin by thinking about your surroundings and the places where you spend most of your time. What are they like and how do you feel when you're there? If you immediately experienced a sense of dread or weariness, there may be room for improvement in your spaces. This doesn't mean you have to go full-blown HGTV to improve your space.

But if Joanna Gaines calls and tells you she's available, you should definitely welcome her in to transform your space.

Let's start with the space where you spend a significant amount of time, your home. When creating a healing environment, there are a handful of features to consider, including the color, lighting, air quality, temperature, artwork, sounds, and natural elements. These aspects of your space can either enhance your ability to relax, or they can increase the likelihood that you'll regularly experience stress.

Colors impact the way you think and feel and can even influence your appetite and metabolism. Colors within healing spaces should encourage a sense of calm and serenity. Cool blues are relaxing colors that have a calming effect on the mind and body. Earthy browns are comforting, often used to make a room feel more soothing and inviting. Green is considered a refreshing color that signifies life, health, and vitality. Deep purples offer a sense of peace and tranquility. Using a combination of a couple of these colors as paint options and in the design features, such as pillows, curtains, or rugs, is a simple way to help a healing space begin to take shape.

A well-lit environment can greatly influence your health and well-being, boosting your energy levels, improving your mood, and positively impacting your mental, emotional, and physical health.

Healing spaces with windows that offer natural light can make time spent in the space more impactful. Natural light produces endorphins (the feel-good hormones), causes the body to produce vitamin D and the brain to produce serotonin (a hormone that helps alleviate pain), provides energy to the body, and makes you feel rested.

If natural light isn't an option, artificial lighting can also be beneficial, helping to lighten your mood, especially when it mimics natural lighting.

Use light dimmers for early morning or late evening time spent in healing spaces. This will benefit your circadian rhythms, the production and regulation of hormones such as serotonin and melatonin, and your sleep cycle.

The air quality within your space will impact your breathing as well as how you feel. Indoor air pollution sources release particles and gasses into the air, which can find their way into your lungs. Improving your air quality can be done through prevention, buying eco-friendly products that release fewer pollutants and are not as harmful to the environment, ventilation, opening doors and windows to allow fresh air to flow in and stagnant air to flow out, and filtration, using devices that clean the air, trap particles, and improve air quality.

You also want to know, and adjust, the humidity levels in your home. Humidity levels that are too high can cause mold to grow. While humidity levels that are too low can lead to dry skin and sinus issues. Ideally, humidity levels should be between 30 and 40 percent.

The temperature of your space influences your comfort and your health. Studies show that temperatures that are too low can cause dampness, which leads to mold and respiratory symptoms. While temperatures that are too high cause stress on the body and exacerbate diabetes and cardiovascular, respiratory, and kidney diseases. The temperature of an indoor space is often influenced by the climate you live in. Aiming for a temperature range of 69–73 degrees Fahrenheit will ensure that your space remains out of the extreme hot and cold zones that negatively impact health and healing.

Your selection of artwork will reflect your preferences. Choosing pieces that are peaceful, serene, and provide you with a sense of tranquility will help with the healing qualities of the space. Images of nature, including plants and water, abstract art, and clean minimalist pieces can create an organic feel and make great additions to relaxing spaces.

Soft, relaxing music enhances time spent in a healing environment. Nature sounds such as waterfalls, ocean waves, and rainfall are extremely beneficial, calming the mind and body and deepening your sense of relaxation.[5]

Including music from sound bowls in your healing space can increase meditative and peaceful states, calm the nervous system, and engage your relaxation response.

Adding plants to your space boosts oxygen levels, stimulates your senses, and heightens the therapeutic value of your space. Plants can also help you heal faster, lower blood pressure, lessen pain, and decrease anxiety.

Indoor water features are soothing, create a spa-like atmosphere, and promote relaxation. They can also improve sleep quality, enhance your décor, and double as humidifiers as they add to the moisture in the space.

Location of your healing environment. When creating a healing environment within your home, choose a space where you'd like to unwind and return to again and again. This is the space to begin the transformation. The size of the space doesn't matter. Even small spaces can offer huge therapeutic benefits.

And as you begin this process I hope you find relief in knowing that all of our homes are well lived in. Your home, where you do the work of tending to family, taking care of guests, and thoughtfully utilizing your spaces and belongings, is not meant to be a showroom. There will be messes, spills, and piles that need tending to, and as long as the real, whole living doesn't interfere with your ability to relax, or see the Son in your midst, you can continue to navigate the seasons where things aren't picturesque. Believing that your home should be magazine ready at all times creates another layer of undue stress, while knowing that you can have spaces dedicated to relaxation can bring you great peace.

Your ability to transform your workspace depends on what type of workspace you have. If you work in your home, you have greater flexibility in the design features and can create a space that keeps you calm and fosters productivity.

If you work in a shared space, you may consider healing elements on a smaller, more personal scale. Incorporating small plants and art features and wearing headphones to listen to soothing music can maintain a sense of relaxation even as you work.

Creating the space is great, but remember that you actually need to be present in the healing environment you create in order to experience the relaxing benefits, so be intentional about spending time there.

How to practice ecotherapy. God created the earth we inhabit, so when we spend time in nature, we bear witness to his masterpiece. We get an immersive encounter with the sights, sounds, and smells of his living, moving artwork, touching and sometimes tasting wonders deliberately handcrafted by God. We also get to enjoy the beauty and honor our symbiotic relationship with the world around us, as everything we need, from the water we drink to the food we eat and the air we breathe, is found in nature. Nature inherently gives us life, so it's no wonder that there are therapeutic benefits to ecotherapy.

Ecotherapy is the practice of spending time outdoors, connecting with nature. Spending just twenty minutes a day or about two hours a week in nature can significantly increase your health and well-being, reducing cortisol levels, relaxing the body, decreasing blood pressure, heart rate, muscle tension, anxiety, depression, pain, postoperative recovery time, and the demands on our cardiovascular system. Ecotherapy can also improve your mood, attention, sense of confidence, and self-esteem, and increases one's ability to be more empathetic and compassionate. Even viewing scenes of nature has this therapeutic effect. This relaxing and restorative practice brings a sense of calm and provides a space for us to spiritually connect with ourselves and our Creator.

Ecotherapy can include walking or other outdoor exercise, gardening (indoors or out), playing with animals, or engaging with natural elements and decorative features while indoors.

Another way to practice ecotherapy is through a technique called grounding, or earthing, which involves direct contact between the human body and the surface of the Earth. Touching the surface of the Earth with your hands or feet connects you to Earth's natural electric charge and surface electrons, allowing these electrons to flow throughout the body, decreasing inflammation and oxidative stress and offering a natural antioxidant effect.[6]

Grounding reduces pain and stress while increasing the speed of wound healing.[7] It also appears to shift the autonomic nervous system from sympathetic toward parasympathetic activation, improve sleep, and increase the number of circulating neutrophils and lymphocytes, the white blood cells that help your immune system fight infection and disease and heal injuries.

One way to engage your relaxation response using ecotherapy is to choose a twenty-minute span of time during your day to spend outside. Next, choose an activity that you're interested in doing while you're outside, which can be some form of play, exercise, or stillness. Then set an alarm and go outside. If you're able to spend even more time with natural elements, feel free to do so. There are no limits to this practice, as you'll continue to experience the benefits of interacting with nature.

Another way to engage your relaxation response using the eco-therapy practice of grounding is to simply take your shoes off and stand on the soil or sand for ten to twenty minutes to experience the benefits. You can also lie down on the Earth's surface, or place your hands in the soil or sand for the same effect.

Animal therapy, which involves interaction with animals as a way to relax, cope with, and recover from some types of physical, mental, and emotional conditions, can be considered another form of ecotherapy. Being in the presence of animals or pets brings a sense of comfort and companionship, decreasing stress and generating a relaxation response.

Typically, dogs, cats, and horses are used in animal therapy, although you can also find other animals such as goats, llamas, and alpacas used in combination with yoga as a stress-relieving technique.

One way to practice animal therapy is to visit a pet store or humane society and engage with the animals. You can also go to the park and watch birds and squirrels, go to a pond or river and watch the wildlife there, or visit any other natural animal habitat and safely observe them.

PRAYER

Lord, the heavens declare your glory, and the skies proclaim the work of your hands. What an awe-inspiring gift it is to behold all that you've created. Meet us as we dwell in holy places and navigate the world around us. And let our lives reflect our time spent communing in your presence. In Jesus' name, amen.

8

Renew Your Mind

IT WAS MY FIRST TIME visiting this care provider's office, and I could feel my pulse racing within me. To look at me, you wouldn't know that I was panicking on the inside. I had grown accustomed to remaining calm even in highly stressful and traumatic situations. But my exam quickly revealed to my new nurse practitioner that something else was going on. "Your pulse is really high Mrs. Braylock. Is everything all right?"

The truth was, I was terrified. I had spent the last few years at home, caring for my young children and working from my laptop. During those long days, and even longer nights, I hadn't spent much time taking care of myself the way I used to. Exercise was sporadic, sitting for long periods of time was common, and having three children under four—with a husband who worked full time and was in grad school—meant that many of my days were brimming with exhaustion. I'd convinced myself that something dreadful would be found because of my own neglect, and my vital signs revealed the depth of my fear.

"I was just in a rush to get here," I told her, too embarrassed to tell her what I was really thinking. And though I'm pretty sure she wasn't convinced by my words, she graciously continued the exam, assuring me that she'd take my blood pressure and pulse again later in the appointment.

After learning that everything looked normal, the immense fear that I had allowed to creep in went away. And when she took the measurements again, everything was within a normal range. I had allowed my thoughts to get the best of me as I believed something about myself without any proof or validity.

You see, your thoughts are so powerful, and are constantly communicating with your body, whether or not what you're believing is the truth. Proverbs 12:25 says, "Anxiety weighs down the heart, but a kind word cheers it up." Whether or not anyone is present to check your pulse, take your blood pressure, or acknowledge that the results of these measurements are out of range, the anxiety that's present can weigh you down.

When your thoughts are stressful, the impact they have on your mind, body, and emotions can appear in numerous ways: feeling overwhelmed; experiencing irritability, depression, anxiety, sadness, panic attacks, insomnia, problems concentrating, fatigue, loneliness, changes in appetite; practicing avoidance of others, isolation, and impulsive and addictive behaviors; having a lack of interest in activities that you previously found enjoyable; and experiencing burnout. You can feel as though you've lost control, feel more emotional than usual, and struggle with keeping track of things and remembering.

INFLUENTIAL WORDS

My love for words began when I was a little girl. My elementary school teacher made each student choose a word and decorate it. My word was *spectacular*. It dazzled on the page. I drew squiggly lines, added glitter, and watched this word come to life.

I was a teenager before I realized the real power that words had on me. Sitting on the steps of my home listening to a '90s R&B song on a cassette tape in my Walkman, I felt a deep sense of sadness come over me. I didn't really understand why, but I turned the music off and almost instantly felt better.

Wait . . . what just happened? Could the words used to describe the pain and heartache of this singer cause a reaction within me?

This was my aha moment. As fascinated as I was with words, I had never considered their potential negative impact on me. These lyrics were influencing my thinking and making me feel terrible about an experience that I was too young to even understand. It was then that I began to consciously think about what I think about.

The Bible says, "See to it that no one takes you captive through hollow and deceptive philosophy, which depends on human tradition and the elemental spiritual forces of this world rather than on Christ" (Colossians 2:8). Yet if we are not careful or conscious about the words, music, news, media, voices, and perspectives we consume, we can regularly allow meaningless and harmful things to invade our thoughts and occupy the space meant for God and his Word to dwell. In doing so, we open the door for invaders and welcome in content, criticism, and commentary designed to imprison and stress our minds.

And though we know there are plenty of outside influences just waiting to take our minds captive, we must also consider the thoughts that arise in our own minds.

THOUGHTS AND THINKING

A thought is an idea, belief, or opinion that occurs in the mind. Thoughts occupy mental space and can appear suddenly, or they can be produced by thinking. Thinking is the conscious directing of one's mind to consider, reason, produce, and connect thoughts. Thinking helps you understand, make judgments, and solve problems. But thoughts aren't always right or the truth, so you can't trust or believe everything you think.

Under certain conditions, like stress, your thoughts can become hazardous to you and those in your presence. Stressful thoughts can distort reality, disregard truth, and become dangerous objects bouncing around in your mind. They can also pull you toward perspectives and problems that are detrimental to your health and your relationship with God, yourself, and others. Stressful thoughts can't be trusted as reliable, nor should they be used as an accurate lens to view your life or the world. And as a believer, you must constantly, and consciously, remove your stressful thoughts so that you can think clearly and in alignment with God.

SELF-DIAGNOSED WITH FEAR AND FALSE IDENTITIES

I paced back and forth in an airport terminal. My willingly adopted fear of heights had a grip on me and was impacting an experience I truly wanted to enjoy. As I sat across from my best friend waiting to board the plane, I felt the fear coming. It began rising from seemingly nowhere, ushering in a sense of panic and causing my body to react to this illusion of danger.

My heart raced. My breathing quickened, and I couldn't sit still anymore. I told my best friend and travel partner that I'd be back and started my fast-paced escape through the concourse, attempting to regain control over what I was feeling.

I desperately wanted to be free, to no longer be gripped by what I was imagining and to experience the truth found in the Word of God.

You see, unaddressed fear will begin to show up as anxiety, where you're no longer fearful of one specific thing, but instead fearful of the world around you. This can happen because your original experience of fear was meant to result in a cry for help, but if you didn't cry out for help, or if your cries for help were not met with a sense of comfort or safety, your fear can become ingrained within you. Which can lead to this perpetual internal cry for help expressing itself as chronic anxiety.

I had clung to this fear of heights for so long that I needed help to let it go. And I only experienced freedom after doing what we find in Psalm 34:4: "I sought the LORD [on the authority of his Word], and he answered me; he delivered me from all my fears."

As I walked, I repeated various verses about fear and anxiety: 2 Timothy 1:7 and Philippians 4:6-7 flowed from my lips.

After a while, my pace and heart slowed. I embraced the truth God prescribed to me instead of clinging to the self-diagnosis of fear that inhibited me from experiencing his joy and peace.

As we boarded the plane, I considered what life could be like if I consistently identified with God's truth. How much freer could I be? Dear friend, pause for a moment to examine the false identities you have aligned yourself with. Do you recognize your old condition—the labels, diagnoses, fears, anxieties, worries, self-dependence, circumstances, and stressful thoughts you're clinging to—that is standing between you and full deliverance?

By God's mercy, you have been healed, set free, and given a new nature. You no longer have to identify with anything other than God's truth—especially not the self-inflicted, wounded identities you have adopted.

You are not your hurt, fear, anxiety, diagnosis, or circumstance. And God is waiting for you to align your thoughts with his thoughts, your words with his words, and your identity with the identity he sacrificed his only begotten Son for you to have. Don't allow stressful thoughts to cause you to forget who you are or prevent you from fully embracing your new identity.

When your beliefs don't line up with your actions, cognitive dissonance occurs—like believing that God is my protector while simultaneously being afraid of not being protected while on the plane. These two thoughts were warring against each other, causing a mental conflict that often results in anxiety, a physical stress response, and spiritual disharmony.

James 1:8 tells us that a double-minded person is unstable and restless in all they do—the way they think, feel, and decide—and should not expect to receive anything from the Lord. Ouch!

The good news is that becoming aware of cognitive dissonance is a motivator to restore harmony in all areas of your life. Acknowledging which thought is the truth (God is my protector) and which is not (I need to fear heights) gives me the option to choose the truth, eliminating the conflict and restoring the harmony I'm intended to embody.

THE UNCAPTURED MIND

Nurses don't always get all the details in emergency situations. You try your best to prepare for anything, to have empathy for patients, and to ready equipment and surgical instruments. So when I was paged and told to get the operating room ready, that's what I did.

After setting up the room, I decided to go to the front desk to check on the status of the case, but I didn't make it there. The patient was already being wheeled toward me. And to my surprise, they were handcuffed to the stretcher, with a police officer following.

I was taken aback. These were circumstances I hadn't experienced before, but there was no time to stop and stare. I gathered myself, accepting that this patient needed surgery and adjusting to accommodate the patient and police officer.

Whatever had taken place prior to their arrival, this person was deemed a threat that required restraint and supervision. The handcuffs and law enforcement presence were a visual indication that the patient could harm themselves and those present to care for them. Safety measures needed to remain in place for everyone involved in this operation.

While the deep wounds on this person's body would leave scars forever testifying to what had taken place that day, I was also left with the imprints of my thoughts surrounding this case. The most relevant being, what happens to us as believers when we neglect to take each thought captive?

In 2 Corinthians 10:5 we're told to take captive every thought to make it obedient to Christ, which tells us a few things. Our thoughts can be disobedient to the Word of God. They can be out of alignment with the truth and, if left uncaptured, can wreak havoc in our lives. Also, safety measures need to be implemented toward the thoughts we think. Yes, our thoughts—the stressful ones, the secret ones, the shame-filled ones, and the seemingly sweet and innocent ones—are incredibly powerful and potentially harmful. Allowing them to roam freely could wound you and those around you. I don't know about you, but I don't want to risk the damage my unbound thoughts could cause. I don't want my thoughts to render everything and everyone in my life scarred. So like the officer standing guard, I will keep watch over my thoughts, subduing whatever is against the truth of God, preventing my thoughts from causing further harm, so they can obey and fit the structure of life shaped by Christ.

REWIRING YOUR BRAIN

One of the most startling and, for many scientists, difficult-to-accept discoveries about the brain occurred in the 1990s. Until then, it was believed that babies were born with all the brain cells they would ever have, and all you could look forward to was gradual mental deterioration as brain cells died off and were never replenished. We now know that the brain is ever evolving, adding new cells, forming new neural pathways, capturing new memories, and transforming in structure—and your thoughts directly influence this process.

When you become saved and God reconciles your relationship, ending the estrangement caused by original sin, a spiritual, mental, and physical transformation takes place and you are now a new creation, causing the old to pass away and your new identity to come into existence (2 Corinthians 5:17).

You are then called to live in accordance with this new identity, so you begin to read the Word of God, learn about God's character, evaluate everything from a divine perspective, and have the mind of Christ (1 Corinthians 2:16)—the capacity to think Christ's thoughts so that you can live as you ought to, reflecting your mental transformation.

Romans 12:2 tells you to be transformed by the renewing of your mind, indicating your ability to participate in your mental transformation, which is both an intangible, spiritual transformation that merges your thoughts with God's and a tangible transformation that rewires the physical structure of your brain. Changes and adaptations to your brain over the course of your life are inevitable, yet you get to influence how it changes.

To ensure that you carry out the spiritual act of renewing your mind and the physical act of rewiring your brain, the Bible tells us, "Do not be anxious about anything, but in every situation, by prayer and petition, with thanksgiving, present your requests to God" (Philippians 4:6). This means that the moment a worrisome thought enters your mind, you are to immediately communicate with God through prayer, making specific requests and drawing on spiritual resources to change your mental direction, physical state, and spiritual posture. And this stops the stress response in its tracks. You are to do this with thanksgiving because in doing so, you demonstrate your faith in God's provision regardless of what you're faced with, which also allows your relaxation response to kick in.

Philippians 4:8 goes on to tell you to think on whatever is true, noble, right, pure, lovely, admirable, excellent, or praiseworthy, and Joshua 1:8 reminds us to meditate, or focus our thoughts, on the Word of God day and night. You're instructed to do this to root the Word of God deeply into your soul so that you're driven by God's perspective, and obedience to these instructions influences your brain's neuroplasticity and epigenetics.

Neuroplasticity is the brain's ability to reorganize, change physiological or structural properties in response to internal or external factors, and function differently than how it previously functioned. Epigenetics is how environmental influences affect gene expression. Epigenetic changes can turn genes on or off and change how your body reads your DNA sequence; some epigenetic changes can be added or removed in response to changes in your environment or behavior.

What does this mean? You will still look like your mother, father, or great-grandparents because your DNA sequence is unchanged, but what you think, say, do, and express can now resemble your heavenly Father and the mind-body-spirit connection and transformation taking place in your life.

This is the modern neuroscientific explanation of how you can follow the instructions of Romans 12:2: "Do not conform to the pattern of this world, but be transformed by the renewing of your mind." Your brain changes as you renew your mind, helping you to respond differently to stress and increase your ability to embody and exhibit the thoughts of God.

ADDITIONAL TIPS FOR RENEWING YOUR MIND

Renewing your mind and changing your thought patterns and habits is a process that can take time and effort, so here are a few tips to get you started:

1. *Identify your negative thought patterns,* such as negative self-talk, self-doubt, or a fear of failure. These can hold you back and make transformation more difficult.

2. *Replace negative thoughts with positive ones.* This can be done by consciously challenging negative thoughts and replacing them with the truth of the Word of God and positive affirmations.[1]

3. *Create new habits.* This may involve things like practicing mindfulness, setting goals, or engaging in positive self-talk.

4. *Practice self-care.* Taking care of yourself is an important part of renewing your mind, cultivating your neuroplasticity, and making your brain more pliable to rewiring. Self-care can include reducing stress; engaging in activities that challenge the brain, like learning a new language or skill; doing physical exercise, which increases blood flow to the brain; getting adequate sleep; and eating foods that support brain function, such as blueberries, nuts, and leafy greens.

Remember, renewing your mind and rewiring your brain is a process, but with dedication and persistence, you can create new thought patterns and habits that will help you relax, reflect God, and live a more fulfilling life.

Let's Relax

RELEASE

Which thoughts have been causing you stress? How can you challenge these thoughts with truth?

When do you most struggle in your thinking? When you're fearful, tired, feeling disconnected from God or others?

REESTABLISH

The mind governed by the flesh is death, but the mind governed by the Spirit is life and peace. (Romans 8:6)

Do not conform to the pattern of this world, but be transformed by the renewing of your mind. Then you will be able to test and approve what God's will is—his good, pleasing and perfect will. (Romans 12:2)

Finally, brothers and sisters, whatever is true, whatever is noble, whatever is right, whatever is pure, whatever is lovely, whatever is admirable—if anything is excellent or praiseworthy—think about such things. (Philippians 4:8)

RECEIVE

How to practice mindfulness for relaxation. In Philippians 2:1-5, Paul reminds Christians to be mindful, doing nothing out of selfish ambition, cultivating unity in the body of Christ. As a practice, *mindfulness* is being aware of the present moment, developing a nonjudgmental attitude toward one's thoughts, feelings, and emotions, and becoming intentional about being Christlike.

Mindfulness can be practiced in many ways. One form of mindfulness is mindful breathing, focusing your attention on the natural rhythm and flow of your breath while acknowledging the source of it. Mindful eating involves using all of your senses to experience your food, listening to your body's clues about hunger and satiety, and giving thanks for God's provision. Mindful walking involves being aware of your mind, body, spirit, and emotions as you move through your environment.

These mindful practices engage your senses, ground you in the present moment, reduce negative thoughts, improve relationships, and can help to reduce stress, improve concentration, and increase self-awareness and self-compassion. Practicing mindfulness can help to reduce anxiety and depression, as well as improve overall physical and mental health.

Mindfulness is a practice that can be done anywhere and anytime. It can be done alone or in a group setting. It's important to remember that mindfulness is a journey and that it takes time and practice to develop. With dedication and commitment, anyone can learn to be mindful and reap the benefits of this practice.

You can engage your relaxation response through the practice of mindful walking. The goal of this practice is to move your body in a way that's both comfortable and effective in supporting your health and relaxation. This practice will help you bring your attention to the present moment, as you become aware of your surroundings, how your body feels, and the thoughts you're thinking as you move.

Your mindful walking practice can easily be modified to a prayer walk, as you pray for whatever is on your heart or praise God for what you're seeing and experiencing, the air you're able to breathe, the ability to move your body, the sand, the trees, the mountains, or whatever may be in your environment. Mindful walking cultivates a practice of glorifying God with your mind, body, and spirit and enables you to reap the benefits of a healthful, relaxing practice.

To begin, center your thoughts on God as you start your walk. Notice how you feel, the pace of your breath, the sounds that surround you, the smells in the air. This is the start of your mindful walking practice. As you practice regularly, you'll continue to deepen your awareness and appreciation for the presence of God all around you and naturally activate your relaxation response.

How to use affirmations for relaxation. An affirmation is a positive statement that helps you challenge and overcome negative thinking, self-doubt, and self-sabotage.

Practicing self-affirmation activates the reward centers in your brain, waking up and increasing neural pathways, changing the way the brain responds to the messages it receives, and increasing positive feelings and happiness. Affirmations can help you decrease stress, increase relaxation, and choose healthier, more beneficial lifestyle options.

Because affirmations can teach and rewire your brain to think in a new way, consciously repeating phrases that convince your brain that you will live a relaxed life causes your brain to subconsciously seek out signs that reinforce this belief. Your brain will then work consciously and subconsciously to help you achieve your goal of a more relaxed life.

Here are a few affirmations to help you activate your relaxation response:

- I embody relaxation.
- With every breath, peace washes over me.
- I release all tension from my body.
- I become more calm with each passing moment.
- I am safe, and I am loved.
- I am relaxed and focused on the blessings in my life.

Scriptures also act as affirmations, aligning your thoughts with God and rewiring your brain to recognize and achieve the biblical truth you're affirming.

You will keep in perfect peace those whose minds are steadfast, because they trust in you. (Isaiah 26:3)

Return to your rest, my soul, for the Lord has been good to you. (Psalm 116:7)

In peace I will lie down and sleep, for you alone, LORD, make me dwell in safety. (Psalm 4:8)

Surely your goodness and love will follow me all the days of my life, and I will dwell in the house of the LORD forever. (Psalm 23:6)

PRAYER

Dear God, thank you for our sound minds, for the ability to choose to think about whatever is true, and lovely and excellent, and to be transformed each time we meditate on your Word. Govern our minds so that we can experience life and peace, and have our minds set on what the Spirit desires. Allow us to continue filling our minds with your living Word and scriptural truth. In Jesus' name, amen.

9

Refuel Your Body

FOOD IS AN INGREDIENT THAT BINDS US TOGETHER, making life a delicious experience and mealtime, potentially, a work of art. Food is considered any nutritious substance that one eats or drinks in order to sustain life, growth, or vital processes. But how often do we pause to truly consider what we're putting into our bodies?

In Genesis 1:29 we read, "Then God said, 'I give you every seed-bearing plant on the face of the whole earth and every tree that has fruit with seed in it. They will be yours for food.'" Yet with all our modern capabilities, we have generated additional options. We manufacture synthetic, laboratory-produced foodlike substances. We consume artificial food additives and substances that have no real nutritional value. We remove the seeds meant to reproduce the very plants we were given by God himself. And then we wonder . . . We wonder why our bodies are racked with pain, why incurable diseases exist and persist, and how it's even possible, with a God as mighty as our own, to experience the debilitating conditions we endure.

We demand answers. We give away the blame. We question God's healing power, our own faith, and the degrees that hang on the walls of our practitioners' offices. Yet we're still not checking for what we're putting in our bodies.

Don't get me wrong. Nobody loves chocolate more than I do. These words aren't meant to shame you or send you to your pantry to throw away everything and start over. But they are meant to serve as a wake-up call for those not paying attention. Blindly consuming delectable advertisements and overflowing plates of substances you may not need or receive any nutritional benefit from just may be part of the reason your stress seems out of control.

And yes, I'm well aware that not every condition we face is food-related or -initiated. Yet our body's ability to prevent, fight against, and heal diseases can be heavily influenced by the foods we eat, so paying attention to what we're consuming is essential.

LIFESTYLE PRACTICES

As a nursing student, I worked nights on the weekends, Friday to Sunday. Going to school full time during the day, then throwing my body and mind into reverse as I demanded that they stay awake at night was not an easy task. My body wanted to sleep at the same time every day, whether or not I was working. So when a heavy sleepiness would begin to rest upon me during my shift, I'd go into the break room and have a snack. Graham crackers, hot tea, saltine crackers, chicken broth, single-serving packets of peanut butter. Whatever it would take to attempt to trick my body into believing that it was supposed to be awake. The waking momentum from snacking never lasted that long, though, and my body would again remind me that it wanted to rest. This type of eating wasn't out of hunger. This type of eating wasn't necessarily nourishing my body. This type of eating was only mindful in the sense that I was intentionally eating as my failing attempt to stay awake.

These types of lifestyle practices, and the use of food as a bargaining tool, contribute to food-fueled stress, disorienting our bodies and causing them more stress. So let's look at some additional ways what we consume, or don't consume, fuels our stress.

Inflammation. A normal bodily response to injury or infection, inflammation occurs when damaged tissues release chemicals that communicate to our white blood cells that they need to start repair work. But low-grade inflammation can spread throughout the body and become a chronic condition. Chronic low-grade inflammation can cause cellular injury, damage the body, and initiate diseases such as rheumatoid arthritis, diabetes, and heart disease.

So how does the food we eat affect inflammatory processes in our bodies? Some of the things we eat (such as fried foods, sugary beverages, processed meats, and shortening or margarine) are known to be inflammation producers as they release inflammatory messengers called cytokines, which raise the risk of chronic inflammation.

High fat. Eating a diet high in fat manipulates the microorganisms in your gut as well as your eating behavior. Typically, when you're hungry your small intestine releases ghrelin, the hunger hormone, which signals the brain either by traveling through the bloodstream or by stimulating the vagus nerve in the gut, which then communicates directly with the brain. When you're full, your small intestine releases appetite-suppressing hormones to turn off the system. However, the low-grade inflammation caused by stress and high-fat diets disrupts and numbs the satiety response in the hypothalamus and the satiety sensors located on the vagus nerve. So inflammation alters the inner workings of your brain and appetite regulation.

High sugar. Diets high in sugar have been linked to higher levels of inflammation and cognitive decline disorders such as Alzheimer's and dementia. A high-sugar diet can also hinder collagen repair, leading to premature wrinkles, reducing the skin's elasticity, and causing poor wound healing.

Excessive sugar intake also disrupts the intestinal barrier, causing profound imbalances in the microbial environment of the gut, changing the way the microbiome functions as well as the metabolic activity, increasing gut permeability and susceptibility to infection.[1]

Food emulsifiers. These are food additives that encourage immiscible substances like oil and water to mix. Although there are more natural emulsifiers such as guar gum and lecithin, which pose few health risks when consumed in normal or small amounts, food emulsifiers can generally decrease the diversity of the gut microbiome and translocate bacteria through the epithelium in the gut barrier, inducing inflammation.

So if we continue to eat foods that are unsuitable for our digestive systems, we should expect to continue to experience the resulting stress.

Dehydration. Dehydration can cause stress, and stress can cause dehydration. When the body is dehydrated, cortisol levels increase while your brain's production of serotonin decreases. Dehydration can cause the buildup of waste and acids in the body, sap your brain of energy, and impact your body's ability to regulate heat. Even mild dehydration can alter your mood, impact your ability to concentrate, lead to a loss of strength and stamina, and put you at higher risk for depression and anxiety symptoms. It's also important to note that one of the physical triggers of panic attacks is dehydration.

Dehydration symptoms may include an increase in hunger as the body seeks other ways to obtain fluids, headaches, weak or cramped muscles, dry mouth, bad breath, cloudy thinking, rapid or shallow breathing, dark-colored urine, little to no urine, extreme thirst, sleepiness, fatigue, or becoming dizzy or lightheaded easily.

With all these potential problems, you might be thinking, why would anyone *not* drink water? Well, it happens quite regularly, and I'd completely understand if you paused for a moment to drink some water.

STRESS-FUELED DIGESTION

Because your gut has hundreds of millions of neurons and is in constant communication with the brain, stress readily affects this brain-gut communication. Changes in gut bacteria caused by stress can then influence your mood.

Stress can increase the occurrence and severity of heartburn. And intense stress can trigger a rare but possible spasm in the esophagus that's usually mistaken for a heart attack. Stress can also make it difficult to swallow some foods.

If your stress is severe enough, it could cause vomiting and unnecessarily alter appetite. Stress, the changes that occur in your body because of it, and the attention placed on the stressor may cause you to lose your appetite or tune out from your hunger cues. Or the opposite may occur. The release of cortisol in response to stress may increase your appetite and cause you to overeat, and you may also experience an increase in cravings, usually for fatty and sugary foods.

Stress often affects the pace at which food moves through your body, resulting in either constipation or diarrhea, so even if you're eating healthy, nutritious foods, your body may not be absorbing the vitamins, minerals, and nutrients you need. Stress also affects the nutrients that the intestines are able to absorb and weakens the intestinal barrier, allowing gut bacteria to enter the body.

REFUEL

I could hear a patient venting his frustrations from several rooms away. As I walked down the hall toward the commotion, I could hear him asking for something different than the day before. He was making it loud and clear that he didn't want the hospital food, and that day, refused to even take the lid off his plate. What he was struggling to care about was that the hospital food had been specifically chosen and portioned to support his healing and recovery. Based on his health condition, the food he was being offered would supplement any nutrient deficiencies, minimize his salt intake, and combat some of the harmful effects of his diet.

Hospital meal plans can be difficult to adjust to, as it's not easy to instantly shift from the wide variety of foods that you've grown to love, whether or not they have much of a health benefit, toward foods that strictly serve a nutritional purpose, even if they have the potential to prolong your life. However, in order to begin decreasing the amount of stress your body is both experiencing and producing, adjusting your food and water intake may be exactly what you need. So let's explore the various ways you can begin to refuel and relax your body from the inside out.

EAT NUTRITIOUSLY

There are many things that are labeled as food, with beautiful packaging and bountiful promises, trying to convince you that you're in need of it. Yet most of them leave you unsatisfied, malnourished, and craving more. Cravings can indicate that something is lacking from your diet, typically in the form of essential vitamins and minerals.

I'm not telling you to eliminate every tasty indulgence from your life. I'm telling you to become aware of what you're putting in your body. Be intentional about what you consume so that you are fueled, your energy is sustained, and you can maintain your health throughout your lifetime.

One way to become more aware of what you're eating is to develop a nutrition plan. Creating a nutrition plan that's realistic, and that you're willing and able to stick to, is important. To do this, begin by assessing what you're already eating. Take a look around your kitchen. What food do you have at home? Begin to notice when you eat. Is it approximately the same time each day? Are you already hungry when you eat? Are your meals planned out in advance? The answers to these questions will make you more mindful about what, when, and why you're eating, and can help you consciously make healthier food choices that keep stress at bay and your body nourished and relaxed.

Next, start planning ahead. Grocery lists, meal planners, and food trackers are helpful tools that keep you mindful about how you're feeding your body. Writing down what you want to buy, how you're going to prepare it, and what you ate will help ensure that you're eating nutritiously and being intentional about how you're fueling your body.

Then be sure to shop well. Make sure you're paying attention to whether or not you stick to the items on your list. If you're prone to self-sabotage, grabbing items that don't have much nutritional value or that aren't on your list, consider ordering your food ahead of time via a shopping app. This way you'll have everything you need, and you won't be tempted by the things you don't.

Also, pay attention to when you're eating. Eating nonstop, around the clock can cause your body to process calories less efficiently, disrupt your circadian rhythm, and contribute to weight gain. Eating in rhythm with your body's clock, typically within an eight-to-twelve-hour window, can support nutrient absorption and better align with your metabolism. Eating beyond this window of time also increases your risk for heart disease, obesity, and diabetes.

Intermittent fasting, which alternates cycles of fasting and eating, gives your body time to rest and digest, as it prolongs the period of time between the use of the calories from your last meal and your next meal, enabling the body to begin burning fat.

Finally, plan your meals. Plan out one day's worth of meals and snacks, including the ingredients you'll need to make them. If you've never tried meal planning, this may seem like a tedious process initially. However, knowing ahead of time what foods are available to you and what you can make with those options can keep your nutritional intake on track. You can make your meals in advance if you'd like, storing them appropriately so that they're ready to go when you're ready to eat.

THE BENEFITS OF PLANT-BASED EATING

Plants are a key source of antioxidants, which prevent or reduce damage caused by oxidation, the process in the human body which produces unstable chemicals called free radicals. Antioxidants neutralize free radicals, breaking a chain of reactions that leads to cell damage.

Plants are our sole source of soluble and insoluble fiber, both of which are powerful inflammation reducers. Fiber helps slow digestion, helping you feel full longer, making it easier to eat fewer calories.

Plant-based eating increases your energy, boosting your metabolism and making digestion easier. It can enhance your mood, improve concentration, help to prevent and reverse disease processes in your body, lower the risk of cancer and heart disease, and decrease cholesterol and blood pressure. Plant-based eating also improves immune function and is associated with lower stress, anxiety, and depression.

USING FOOD AS MEDICINE

The food you eat can be considered medicinal depending upon what you're consuming and how you're consuming it. Prioritizing your nutrition and eating foods that will help prevent and treat illness can help you decrease or eliminate chronic conditions and the medications associated with them. Plus, in order for all of your cells to perform their functions at optimal levels, adequate nutrition is necessary.[2] So selecting your foods and creating meals based upon their nutritional content and value can help you target the healthful results you want to achieve.

Choosing anti-inflammatory foods can make a significant impact on your diet and is a natural way to reduce inflammation. Examples of anti-inflammatory foods include healthy oils, herbs, spices, dark berries, leafy greens, cruciferous vegetables, legumes, and nuts. Here is a list of some specific anti-inflammatory foods you can incorporate into your diet.

Blueberries are full of vitamins and antioxidants and help to reduce oxidative stress, ease existing inflammation, and prevent free radicals from triggering new inflammation.

Cherries are packed with antioxidants and help decrease oxidative stress and inflammation.

Sweet potatoes help decrease inflammation as they're loaded with vitamin C and beta carotene, two protective antioxidants.

Dark leafy greens such as spinach, kale, and collard greens are packed with folate, lutein, and vitamin K, decreasing inflammation and slowing cognitive decline.

Avocados contain several vitamins, minerals, antioxidants, and phytochemicals known to decrease inflammation. They also contain monounsaturated fatty acids and are an excellent source of fiber.

Quinoa is a complex carbohydrate that contains an abundance of anti-inflammatory phytochemicals.

Cacao is rich in antioxidants and flavonoids and also beneficial in reducing inflammation. Dark chocolate with 70 percent or more of cacao is a beneficial source of antioxidants, minerals, and anti-inflammatory polyphenols.

Fatty, or oily, fish such as salmon, mackerel, sardines, herring, tuna, trout, swordfish, and anchovies are high in omega-3 polyunsaturated fatty acids. Healthy omega-3 fatty acids turn off the inflammatory response, increase the cells' ability to get rid of harmful or damaged components, and reduce the risk of heart disease, stroke, and brain function decline.

Nuts and seeds have the potential to reduce inflammation and oxidative stress. From almonds and walnuts to pistachios and cashews, nuts have inflammation-reducing properties, including omega-3 fatty acids, phytonutrients, and flavonoids. Chia and flaxseed are also high in omega-3 fatty acids and alpha linoleic acid (ALA).

You can also spice up your meals with inflammation-fighting spices.

Cinnamon has anti-inflammatory properties, lowers glucose levels, reduces cholesterol, and reverses oxidative damage.

Turmeric's anti-inflammatory benefits stem from curcumin, a compound that blocks free radicals from triggering new inflammation and inhibits inflammatory cytokines.

Black pepper has anti-inflammatory and pain-reducing effects, and it enhances the absorption of curcumin.

Red pepper has anti-inflammatory and antioxidant properties. Capsaicin, which is responsible for a red pepper's spicy heat, has the ability to prevent or halt cancer cell growth by inhibiting cancer-related inflammatory compounds.

Cloves have antioxidant and anti-inflammatory properties. The active compound in cloves is eugenol, which suppresses inflammatory pathways to inhibit the progression of asthma, arthritis, and the growth of cancer cells.

Ginger is rich in anti-inflammatory compounds such as gingerols that reduce pain and soothe muscles. Ginger eases joint inflammation associated with arthritis and osteoarthritis.

Rosemary is another rich source of antioxidants and anti-inflammatory compounds.

Black and green tea have anti-inflammatory benefits as well, although the anti-inflammatory properties will vary from one tea to another. Rosehip, holy basil, turmeric, ginger, and cinnamon can also be consumed as tea.

FRUITS AND VEGETABLES

When selecting your produce, choosing a variety of colors ensures that you're getting a good balance of the fiber and nutrients your body needs. The pigments in plants are packed with powerful antioxidants.[3] The main pigments in fruits include flavonoids, carotenoids, and anthocyanins.

Flavonoids are found in the peels of citrus fruits and have antioxidant, antidiabetic, and hypolipidemic properties. This means that they help scavenge free radicals, suppress inflammation, promote apoptosis (the programmed death of a cell or the elimination of cells that contain potentially dangerous mutations), and regulate lipid metabolism—processes involving the digestion, absorption, synthesis, and decomposition of lipids.

It's important to note here that apoptosis is crucial to the body's ability to identify, destroy, and prevent the accumulation of cancerous cells in the body. When too little apoptosis occurs, cancer cells survive longer, giving them more time to mutate and invade other tissue.

Carotenoids (which contribute to the red, yellow, and orange pigments of plants such as tomatoes, pumpkins, apricots, and carrots) have beneficial antioxidant and anti-inflammatory properties, enhance the immune system, and lower the risk for some degenerative disorders.

Anthocyanins (which contribute to the red, blue, and purple pigments in such foods as blueberries, grapes, purple eggplant, red cabbage, cherries, plums, and beets) contain anti-inflammatory, antidiabetic, antimicrobial, and anticancer properties.

WATER

About 60 percent of your body is made up of water, while about 90 percent of your blood is made up of water, and every cell, all of your tissues, and each organ in your body need water to properly function.

Drinking adequate amounts of water can prevent dehydration and the potential resulting mood changes, unclear thinking, constipation, overheating, kidney stones, various skin disorders, premature wrinkling, and the triggering of headaches and migraines.

Here are some tips for drinking more water:

- Fill and carry a reusable water bottle.

- Serve water during meals.

- Adding cucumber slices or lemon wedges to your water can improve the taste and help you drink more.

- Drink water before, during, and after a workout.

- When you feel hungry, first drink water. Thirst is often confused with hunger, and true hunger will not be satisfied by drinking water.

- Drink on a schedule, perhaps setting reminders to notify you throughout the day to maintain the same schedule. Drink water when you wake up, during breakfast, lunch, and dinner, with snacks, and an hour before bedtime.

- Use a chart or an app to track your water intake.

Remember that the benefits of drinking more water are endless because water helps you get rid of toxins, decrease inflammation, lubricate and cushion joints, and restore the body's ability to heal itself. So drink up!

Let's Relax

RELEASE

Would you consider yourself malnourished—over- or undereating, or consistently lacking nutrient-rich foods in your diet?

How does stress impact your appetite and your food and beverage choices?

REESTABLISH

Then God said, "I give you every seed-bearing plant on the face of the whole earth and every tree that has fruit with seed in it. They will be yours for food." (Genesis 1:29)

So whether you eat or drink or whatever you do, do it all for the glory of God. (1 Corinthians 10:31)

RECEIVE

How to practice integrative nutrition for relaxation. Integrative nutrition is a holistic approach to health and wellness that focuses on nourishing the body from the inside out. It's based on the belief that what we eat, drink, and think affects our physical, mental, and emotional well-being. Ecclesiastes 8:15 puts it like this: "So I commend the enjoyment of life, because there is nothing better for a person under the sun than to eat and drink and be glad. Then joy will accompany them in their toil all the days of the life God has given them under the sun."

By combining traditional nutrition with modern science-based research, integrative nutrition helps individuals achieve optimal health through personalized dietary plans and lifestyle changes. An integrative nutritional approach can help you develop a plan to heal your gut, decrease inflammation, and relax your body.

One of the ways you can use integrative nutrition to rehab your relaxation response is to select recipes that are rich in anti-inflammatory ingredients. Consuming foods that reduce inflammation, improve blood flow, and decrease cellular wear and tear increases the body's ability to achieve and sustain a state of relaxation.

To help you get started, here's my favorite anti-inflammatory breakfast smoothie recipe. It's filling, healing, and tastes good too. Plus, it's packed with vitamins, nutrients, and antioxidants to help you relax from the inside out. Simply combine these ingredients in a blender for two minutes, and enjoy.

- 1 cup blueberries
- 3 tsp cacao
- 2–3 tsp liquid stevia
- 2 cups almond milk
- ½ cup ice

How to garden for relaxation. It's no wonder that one can feel relaxed and at home in their garden, tending, harvesting, and experiencing its fullness. The Garden of Eden, the original earthly home inhabited by man and woman, was a heavenly space full of beauty that was pleasing to the eye and food meant to nourish the body.

Today we know that not only can gardening produce a harvest that will help nourish your body, but the practice of gardening can also improve your balance, strength, and flexibility; offer you beauty; increase your physical activity by offering light aerobic exercise as you tend to the soil, pull, dig, and reach for your fruits, vegetables, and herbs; and help you relax.

One of the ways you can begin gardening, indoors or out, is by starting a medicinal herb garden. An herb that contains substances that can be used for therapeutic purposes is considered medicinal. These herbs can be used aromatically or in decoctions, infusions, and recipes.

Herbs with relaxation properties include lavender, chamomile, lemon balm, Saint John's wort, peppermint, rosemary, and holy basil.

Additional medicinal herbs to consider growing in your garden include sage, dill, parsley, echinacea, thyme, mullein, cilantro, ginger, ginseng, turmeric, basil, oregano, and stevia.

Before planting your medicinal garden, consider where you'll grow your herbs.

- Will your garden be indoors or outside?
- Will you plant them in a container or in the ground?

Choose the herbs you want to grow.

- Why do you want an herb garden?
- What remedies do you have in mind?
- What conditions are you trying to prepare for?
- Where do you live? What herbs can handle your climate?

Prepare for your harvest.

- Do you have drying racks, dehydrators, and other products you need to preserve your harvest?

Consult with your care provider.

- Will the herbs you're consuming or placing on your body interfere with any medication or preexisting condition?

How to practice hydrotherapy for relaxation. In the Bible, water is used as a symbol to represent different aspects of God's power, including cleansing (Exodus 30:18), blessing (Jeremiah 17:8), God's ability to refresh (John 4:14), and the fulfillment of God's promises (John 7:38). Amazingly, water is just as powerful in the physical realm as it is in the spiritual realm.

Hydrotherapy is the internal or external use of water in its various forms—water, ice, or steam—to promote relaxation, health, and healing. It can be used to relieve pain, swelling, stiffness, and muscle tension or to increase blood flow and the release of endorphins that relax the body.

Drinking water can help your body relax in several ways. Water transports nutrients, hormones, and chemical messengers to vital organs. So the more hydrated you are, the more effectively your body can produce serotonin, decrease cortisol, improve central nervous system activity, and ultimately calm itself.

Other practical ways to incorporate hydrotherapy into your routine to elicit the relaxation response include bathing in hot or cold water, spending time in a sauna or hot tub, using ice packs or hot water bottles, getting a hydromassage, or participating in floatation therapy, swimming, or water aerobics.

Even listening to the sound of water reduces stress and anxiety, decreases your heart rate, and stimulates the relaxation response. Among the various nature sounds, water is the most effective for soothing.

PRAYER

Lord, thank you for the ability to nourish our bodies, for providing food from the earth that we may eat and enjoy. Guide us in choosing to consume what will give us longevity so that we can continue to serve you and your kingdom. In Jesus' name, amen.

10

Rest Your Body

THERE USED TO BE A SIGN on the street outside of one of our local hospitals that read *Quiet Hospital Zone*, implying that the people inside the hospital would benefit from a minimum level of noise. Once inside the hospital, patients and visitors were also greeted with signs indicating visitation hours, reinforcing that the hospital is a restful environment.

Yet in the past, the patient experience was quite different from what the signs suggested. The nurses' station was a busy, not-so-quiet place with all the phone calls, consultations, and charting going on. And for some, the noise levels inside their rooms weren't much better, with beeping monitors, televisions, roommates, visitors, and a variety of hospital personnel assessing needs day and night. It's not unusual for a patient to request a room away from the nurses' station, especially if they'd spent time in the hospital before. All the activity and varying volumes throughout the stay could make it extremely difficult to get into a rhythm of getting to sleep and staying asleep while in the hospital.

In recent years, many hospitals have made great strides with decreasing the volume and types of sounds heard throughout a hospital stay, recognizing how vital sleep and rest are when one is in need of healing support. It's also important that you begin to pay attention to the volume and types of sounds surrounding you while you're attempting to sleep.

SLEEP DISRUPTORS

Sleep disruptors can include environmental factors, medical conditions, and life circumstances that impede the quantity and quality of sleep you need.

Environmental noise can significantly disrupt sleep. Hearing sounds while you're trying to sleep repeatedly activates your stress response, whether or not you're aware of it, as your brain processes sound even while you're asleep. Night noise pollution caused by transportation like cars, buses, trains, airplanes, and emergency vehicles can be quite troublesome.

Medical conditions can greatly disrupt your sleep as well. Sleep deprivation can then aggravate your condition, causing you to experience more stress, and in turn can generate more sleep disturbances, creating a grueling cycle. Obstructive sleep apnea is an example of such a condition. When we're asleep, our throat muscles relax. For some, this causes the windpipe to narrow or become covered, stopping air from getting in and causing the body to gasp for air. This life-saving reaction that causes one to wake suddenly and repeatedly throughout the night is called obstructive sleep apnea. In severe cases, this process occurs every couple of minutes throughout the night and can leave you feeling worn out the next day. It can also lead to other health issues such as strokes, heart arrhythmia, and high blood pressure.

When a lack of sleep, or disrupted sleep, regularly occurs over several months or years, it's considered insomnia.[1] This medical condition that results in sleeplessness can look like an inability to fall asleep, very light sleep with constant waking with even the slightest disturbance, regularly waking in the night or early morning, being unable to fall back to sleep, or feeling exhausted throughout the day and needing to take frequent naps.

Restless legs syndrome (RLS) is a sleep disorder in which one wakes during the night with itching, crawling, throbbing, or achy sensations in the legs. RLS happens after a period of inactivity, so it's likely to occur before or during sleep. Although RLS is usually temporarily relieved by moving the legs, occurrences can last from fifteen to forty seconds up to an hour or two throughout the night, making it difficult to achieve extended periods of sleep.

Regularly waking up at night with the need to urinate is another medical condition called nocturia. This sleep disturbance can become common as you get older as bladder muscles can weaken and become harder to control. It can also be caused by hormonal changes, urinary tract infections, heart conditions, enlarged prostates, and diabetes.

Jet lag is a type of fatigue that occurs when you travel across different time zones. It can disrupt your circadian rhythm, causing your internal clock to be out of sync and leaving you tired for days.

Pregnancy and the alterations that occur in the body, including pain, heartburn, and nocturia, can make it difficult to get comfortable and remain asleep for long enough to get good quality sleep.

Welcoming a new baby brings a bundle of joy into your life, and usually, disrupted sleep routines. While the baby is learning how to navigate the new world, parents have to navigate sleeping when they can until the baby's sleep schedule is established.

Working the night shift means living, at least temporarily, out of sync with your natural circadian rhythm. Those who work nights are at an increased risk for workplace accidents and can develop sleep disorders over time.

Hosts and house guests alike lose sleep during visits. Whether it's the excitement of being together, the preparations that take place, sleeping in an unfamiliar bed, or trying to match one another's sleep schedule, having a guest or being a guest can disrupt your sleep.

Stress can also initiate and increase patterns of disordered sleeping. It can lead to insomnia, which usually dissipates when the stressful situation ends. However, one's sleep reactivity, the degree to which stress disrupts sleep, can play a huge role in their ability to fall and stay asleep. Those with low sleep reactivity tend to have fewer problems with sleep during stressful times, while those with high sleep reactivity can experience a drastic deterioration of their sleep when they're stressed. High sleep reactivity can precipitate depression, anxiety, and insomnia or increase the risk of negative post-traumatic outcomes.

Sleep reactivity is a bidirectional problem because being exposed to stress can disrupt sleep, and sleep disturbances can increase sleep reactivity, causing additional stress.

Additionally, work-related stress, financial stress, and invisible labor are worth further discussion as they can disrupt your sleep and significantly impact your life.

WORK-RELATED STRESS

The room was dark for this particular surgical procedure, and as I walked around the anesthesia machine, I felt a sharp poke in my leg. I had brushed up against something in a trash bag sitting on the floor.

I looked up at the young resident and said, "There's a needle sticking out of the bag." Even behind his mask I could tell he was terrified. It was atypical for a trash bag to be on the floor or for anything sharp to be present because there's a protocol for sharp objects like needles and glass vials, and a specific container to place them in.

I was flooded with emotions and wrestled with my thoughts as I made the phone call to infection control to tell them what had happened. Although all of the personnel involved were pretty sure that this needle was solely used to draw up medicine, the steps that I had to take following the incident made me question the profession I loved.

The patient would be continuously monitored, and my name would remain on a list for the next several years. If their lab work indicated that the patient had hepatitis B or C, HIV, or any other contagious disease, I would be notified.

There's nothing anyone can say to you to make things better in these moments. In addition to being flooded with emotions, I questioned my life choices and wrestled with my ability to return to this space and work alongside the person that caused these circumstances. Sure, we all make mistakes, but this was a work-related stress that could have been avoided.

Work-related stress is a common issue that can affect anyone, regardless of job or position, resulting from the demands and pressures of work.[2] It can be caused by a variety of factors including long hours and commutes, heavy workloads, poor or dangerous working conditions, lack of job security, conflicts with coworkers, or not enjoying the work you're doing.

Whether you're wrestling with unpleasant working conditions, an unpleasant commute, coworker conflicts, or challenging company culture, work-related stress can wreak havoc on your sleep, disrupting both the quality and quantity of your sleep each night and causing physical symptoms such as headaches, fatigue, and gastrointestinal problems, or mental health issues such as anxiety and depression. Chronic work-related stress can increase the risk of developing certain health problems such as heart disease and diabetes. Work-related stress can also make it difficult to maintain healthy habits, such as regular exercise and good nutrition, further impacting your health.

You can be doing work that you love, but if you're underpaid or you can't live off the salary you're making, this is another form of work-related stress that can impact your sleep, financial health, and overall well-being.

There are two Scriptures that can help you show up with a more relaxed posture as you work toward various solutions: "Do everything without grumbling or arguing" (Philippians 2:14), and "Whatever you do [no matter what it is] in word or deed, do everything in the name of the Lord Jesus [and in dependence on Him], giving thanks to God the Father through Him" (Colossians 3:17 AMP).

It's estimated that the average person will spend 90,000 hours, or one-third of their life, at work, so to the best of your ability, it's wise to spend that time doing work you enjoy. It may take time, prayer, additional education, or a change in employment to experience work that's joyful and fulfilling, so these Scriptures are reminders to do everything as unto the Lord without grumbling or arguing. Heeding these instructions can help ease disappointments, frustration, and stress and increase your peace in the midst of what you're experiencing at work.

FINANCIAL STRESS

I bought myself a new car when I graduated from nursing school—a beautiful navy-blue Mercedes Benz. Everything was going well until I decided to go back to school for my master's degree. Working full time and going to school full time became a bit too much, so I decided to work part time for a while. A decision that didn't leave me with enough money to pay for the car.

But the financial ebbs and flows didn't stop there. From transitioning from full-time nurse to full-time mom, to the feast and famine of budding entrepreneurship and bills that don't stop coming, my finances over the years have been less than ideal and littered with stress. So I know a thing or two about tossing and turning, losing sleep because of less-than-ideal finances.

Financial stress can be experienced by anyone and for a variety of reasons, including job loss, unexpected expenses, debt, and low income. The stress that comes with financial problems can impact your mental and physical health leading to anxiety and depression, as well as other mental health problems, headaches, digestive problems, and of course, difficulty sleeping. Financial stress may also lead to unhealthy coping mechanisms such as overeating, overspending, and substance abuse, which can further exacerbate the stress being experienced. The constant hum in the back of your mind that financial stress can cause as you ruminate from day to day about how you're going to pay your impending bills can also have a similarly stressful impact.

INVISIBLE LABOR

"Hey, where are you?" my husband asked.

"What do you mean? I'm at home," I responded. *I mean, where else would I be?* I thought.

We had three children under four at the time, and I was sure that he knew exactly where we were—at home.

"They have an appointment right now," he said.

"They what?" I yelled.

I couldn't believe that my children had an appointment, and I was completely unaware of it. Not only that. We were late for the appointment, and in no way ready to leave out the door.

I could feel my blood pressure rising. How did I miss this? Would they let us keep the appointment if I couldn't get there right away? How am I going to get these children ready and out the door? There had to be a mistake, and it couldn't possibly be mine. But nevertheless, there I was, breaking out in a sweat and rushing my children out of the house.

Being the keeper of all the dates, times, and appointments for three additional humans had gotten the better of me, and I felt like the world was falling apart. Of course, it wasn't, but it felt that way. Because that's what the invisible workload feels like. A running tally of endless tasks that no one else seems to know exists or takes responsibility for, which weighs heavily on the mind, offering a constant hum in the background of your thoughts that doesn't allow your mind to rest or feel at ease.

Invisible labor is the unpaid work that's done to keep those around you happy and comfortable that often goes unnoticed, unappreciated, and unregulated. It includes tasks such as coordinating family events, scheduling appointments, managing household work and finances, transporting others to and from school, meetings, practices, and appointments, planning vacations, and volunteering at schools, church, and in the community. This invisible labor requires ongoing attention to detail and task management that can be a significant source of stress.

One of the reasons this type of labor can be stressful is because it's often taken for granted, and when these contributions aren't valued or recognized, it can lead to feelings of frustration and resentment. Invisible labor can be time-consuming and take up mental space not visible to others, leading to feeling overwhelmed and burned out. And as you juggle multiple responsibilities with little or no support, you can begin to feel exhausted, like you have no time for self-care, leisurely activities, or your own needs and desires because there is always something else that needs to be done.

This type of stress is prevalent in caregivers (either of young children or those responsible for the care of individuals with a disability or aging family members), in single-parent households, and in entrepreneurship.

Invisible labor can also occur in the workplace with the carrying out of tasks and planning of activities that benefit the company but don't lead to career advancement, including the planning of office parties, and the emotional and relational caregiving of coworkers.

WIDE AWAKE

There are some who think that sleep is overrated, or that less is more, and cut back on sleep in order to accomplish more tasks throughout the day. There are others who are facing financial stress or an invisible workload, and they sacrifice sleep because of stress, working multiple jobs in an attempt to make ends meet or to catch up on laundry and other ongoing housework. This practice may work for a while; however, a lack of sleep will catch up to you. Sleep is your body's way of healing and restoring the energy resources you've used throughout the day. While you're asleep your cells are repaired, your hormones are regulated, and your energy is replenished. If you aren't sleeping well, you're not repairing, regulating, or replenishing well either.

Attempting to cut back on the amount of sleep you need can cause a wide range of problems, including increased pain, injury, heightened stress and emotional responses, hormones that are out of whack, and decreases in your energy, ability to focus, and even your ability to enjoy your everyday life. Insufficient and poor-quality sleep can also trigger stress, have unfavorable effects on your relationships and productivity, and act as a barrier to fully healing stress that's already present.

Plus, God designed your body to require sleep. Psalm 127:2 says, "It is vain for you to rise early, to retire late, to eat the bread of anxious labors—for He gives [blessings] to His beloved even in his sleep" (AMP). We also see in Isaiah 30:15, "This is what the Sovereign LORD, the Holy One of Israel, says: 'In repentance and rest is your salvation, in quietness and trust is your strength, but you would have none of it.'" Here we see that Israel is behaving like rebellious children, refusing to return to God, to rest, or to rely on his promises. They are shunning the power found in repentance and rest, instead of using what they're going through as an opportunity to draw closer to God. I don't know about you, but wasting time ignoring the God-designed requirement of sleep, fleeing from God's presence instead of returning to him, or missing out on some of my blessings because I refuse to rest are not behaviors I want to practice. So if you feel the need to put this book down right now to go take a nap, I'd completely understand.

It's important to note that sleep and rest are not the same. Sleep is a vital natural process, a physical activity and biological necessity critical to the healing and replenishment of the body. While rest is a period of inactivity or a period when you've stopped working or exerting yourself in order to be fully present—mind, body, and spirit. Although different, both are necessary, help to maximize relaxation, and are essential components of God's design for human well-being. The Sabbath rest, as instituted by God, emphasizes the importance of ceasing labor and finding rest in him. This concept extends to all aspects of life, indicating that rest is not just a physical need, but a spiritual discipline that brings renewal and communion with God. Matthew 11:28 is an invitation for believers to find rest in Jesus, displaying that true relaxation comes from spiritual surrender and trust in God.

SLEEP

Adequate sleep quality and quantity are vital to how you navigate each day. Sleep impacts your hormones, your hunger, and even your happiness. This restorative, daily healing practice is often minimized in our world and culture. And while being encouraged to hustle harder, you may start to neglect or decrease the amount of time you spend implementing this basic, essential practice.

Sleep helps improve creativity, problem solving ability, and cognitive skills such as learning, attention, and memory.

So exactly how much sleep do you need? The figure below shows the numbers according to the National Sleep Foundation.[3]

SLEEP DURATION RECOMMENDATIONS

Newborns (0–3 months)	**14–17 hours**
Infants (4–11 months)	**12–15 hours**
Toddlers (1–2 years)	**11–14 hours**
Preschoolers (3–5 years)	**10–13 hours**
School-age children (6–13 years)	**9–11 hours**
Teenagers (14–17 years)	**8–10 hours**
Adults (18–64 years)	**7–9 hours**
Older adults (65 and above)	**7–8 hours**

IMPROVING YOUR SLEEP

If you want to improve your sleep, try keeping a regular sleep routine, going to sleep and waking up at the same time every day. Have a wind-down routine that includes going for a leisurely walk, journaling, or taking a warm bath. Stopping digital device use at least one hour before bedtime can also help to improve your sleep.

The temperature of your room, the clothes (or lack of clothes) you wear, and your bedding impact your body temperature, wakefulness, rapid eye movement, and sleep stages. Becoming intentional about the temperature in your room can help you maximize your sleep quality.

Light exposure throughout the night can negatively impact transitions between sleep cycles, reducing the quality of your sleep and the amount of time you spend in deeper, more restorative sleep stages. Blackout curtains can help significantly with blocking out unwanted light.

Colors influence our emotions, so it's a good idea to pay attention to the colors you have in your bedroom. Keeping your room in the relaxing realm of blue, gray, silver, neutrals, and earth tones can help you achieve a more restful night's sleep. Also, using a flat paint versus a gloss can help reduce light reflection in your bedroom.

Some scents, including rose, lavender, chamomile, jasmine, geranium, and bergamot, promote relaxation, making it easier to fall and stay asleep and experience a more restful night.

Nighttime noise can cause an extra production of hormones such as adrenaline and cortisol and may cause your heart rate and blood pressure to remain elevated. Even if you don't fully awaken, noises can disrupt your sleep cycles, so it's important to try to cancel as much of it as you possibly can. Headphones, earplugs, ambient music, or soundproofing insulation are options that can offer you a more restful night's sleep.

Using earplugs with the highest-level noise reduction rating of thirty-three decibels can significantly decrease sound distractions while you sleep. And soundproofing your room using soundproof curtains can help block soundwaves. Opt for a product that has a sound transmission class (STC) rating of twenty or higher. You can also place a towel or door draft stopper at the bottom of your bedroom door to dampen noise.

Removing clutter, choosing high-quality bed linen, and upgrading your pillows and mattress can have a profound impact on your quality of sleep. Eliminating allergens and broken mattress springs reduces unnecessary aches and pains, also improving how well you sleep.

RELEASE

What stressors are currently keeping you up at night? How are they preventing or distracting you from getting an adequate amount of sleep every night?

Is there something that's impacting your ability to get high-quality sleep? How is your lack of good sleep negatively impacting you throughout your day?

REESTABLISH

> In peace I will lie down and sleep, for you alone, LORD, make me dwell in safety. (Psalm 4:8)

> In vain you rise early and stay up late, toiling for food to eat—for he grants sleep to those he loves. (Psalm 127:2)

RECEIVE

How to breathe for relaxation. God breathed the breath of life into our lungs and sustains each breath we take, so our breathing should not be taken for granted. There are ways to practice breathing that expand our lungs and capacity for more air within them, while simultaneously improving the way our bodies function.

Breathwork and breathing therapy are two integrative practices that focus on using the power of breath to help improve overall health and well-being. Breathwork involves consciously controlling the breath to cultivate a calming and meditative state. Breathing therapy, on the other hand, focuses on using specific breathing techniques to address physical, mental, and emotional distress. Both practices are designed to bring awareness to the breath and how it affects the mind, body, and spirit. With regular practice, breathwork and breathing therapy work to bring more oxygen into the body, reduce stress and inflammation, improve mood, boost the immune system, increase focus and mental clarity, and reduce tension and fatigue.

To use breathwork to elicit the relaxation response, sit comfortably and place one hand on your abdomen. Begin to pay attention to your natural breathing pattern. When you're ready to begin, slowly breathe in through your nose for a count of four, feeling your belly expand as you inhale. Then hold your breath for a count of four. Next, slowly exhale through your nose for a count of four, feeling your abdomen flatten as you release the air. Repeat this practice four or more times, until you feel relaxed.

How to laugh for relaxation. Laughter activates the relaxation response, reduces your stress, improves your mood, eases physical ailments, stimulates many organs, and increases oxygen intake, pain tolerance, and the endorphins released by your brain.

On average, children laugh about four hundred times a day, while adults laugh only about fifteen times. Proverbs 17:22 says, "A cheerful heart is good medicine, but a crushed spirit dries up the bones." So let this be a reminder to laugh more frequently. Laughter has a way of relaxing everything, healing hurts, resentments, and disagreements, lightening our loads, strengthening our bonds, and easing physical, mental, and emotional discomforts.

Smiling and laughter activate mirror neurons in the brain.[4] Mirror neurons fire when you make certain motor functions, and they respond to those same actions observed in others. That's why we say laughing, smiling, and yawning are contagious, or we say someone has an infectious laugh or smile. These actions can be "caught" or mirrored by being near someone who is doing that action.

You can laugh more often by watching a comedic movie. Whether alone or with others, watching a funny movie is inexpensive medicine. You could attend a comedy show, as laughing alongside others can enhance the naturally therapeutic experience. You could also take a laughter yoga class, which combines movement and breathing exercises to promote intentional laughter. Or you could learn some new jokes to keep yourself giggling or share your jokes to brighten up someone else's day. I'll go first. Where's the worst place to hide in a hospital? The ICU. See! A simple way to keep the joy flowing.

PRAYER

Dear God, thank you for soul-restoring rest. Help us, Lord, as we navigate a world full of restless expectations, as you have designed us to require rest to sustain our health and living. Help us to say no, to be still, and to receive the rest we can only find by entrusting our lives to you. In Jesus' name, amen.

11

Recondition Your Body

I ANXIOUSLY STOOD OVER MY FIRSTBORN while he lay in his bassinet. He had spent the last few days fighting off a cold, and the sound of his stuffy breathing made me uncomfortable.

Although he seemed to be returning to his happy, smiley self again, I felt an overwhelming sense of responsibility to monitor him closely. Propping him up as the pediatrician had suggested, I stood there watching him like a mama bear protecting her cub.

As I lingered, his breathing returned to its normal, quiet pattern, but instead of peace, I felt a rush of adrenaline. I then found myself placing my ear close to his nose to make sure he was truly breathing.

Stepping back and breathing a sigh of relief, I received a gentle reminder from God—*You're not keeping him alive.* It was then that I felt the burden lift, which I hadn't realized I'd been carrying, and my true need and desire for rest settled in.

What I thought was my sense of responsibility for my child's life was actually fear of the unknown. It was a fear that caused me to make up horrible possibilities that kept me from focusing on the truth about who God is and what he's capable of. I was there to care for my son, but I was not the one sustaining his life. This role was solely meant for God.

When fears and restlessness place you in a position you're not designed for, you experience the resulting stress and exhaustion, and you deny yourself entrance into the presence of the One who designed my son and me.

Jesus offers an opportunity in Matthew 11:28: "Come to me, all you who are weary and burdened, and I will give you rest." It's an opportunity to surrender and receive the rest your mind, body, and spirit desperately need.

If you're weary, burdened, and stressed because you're carrying loads that were only intended to be in the hands of the Almighty, know that you can return to God at any moment, casting your cares, anxieties, worries, and concerns upon him (1 Peter 5:7) and immediately experience the rest you're needing.

He will relieve you from the disappointments, doubts, and distress you've experienced and relax you with his unwavering love. He's trustworthy, my friend, and able to care for you and whatever you're going through. It's time to stop hanging out with your fears and hovering over your responsibilities. Hand everything over to God so he can heap upon you the rest you need.[1]

YOU CAN'T HEAL WHAT REMAINS HIDDEN

"Is there anything else you'd like to discuss?" the practitioner asked. The young woman was hesitant to speak, and as a student watching the interaction unfold, I wondered how often those who took the time to schedule an appointment refused to share once they were in the office. She had arrived at this clinic alone, which took some courage, but when asked to share more, she couldn't seem to find the words. For whatever reason—fear of judgment, embarrassment, shame—she couldn't seem to allow her questions and desire for help to leave her lips.

The practitioner decided to give her a few more minutes, with the hope that she'd again build up the courage to get what she needed out of the appointment. You see, my friend, you can't heal your stress or get the help you're longing for if you're hiding.

Whether what you're going through requires you to ask questions or to share information that's uncomfortable to disclose, it may be a necessary step toward getting unstuck from the stress you're experiencing. Because not asking for the help you need can lead to unnecessary anger, frustration, weariness, and resentment when the help doesn't come.

Unfortunately, sometimes we wait until we're worn out from trying to hide ourselves and our needs from God before we seek help. Hebrews 4:16 reminds us, "Let us then approach God's throne of grace with confidence, so that we may receive mercy and find grace to help us in our time of need."

So whether you're dealing with a devastating loss, discouraging conversation, disappointing diagnosis, or difficult decision—or if you simply want to delight in God's presence—he will join you on your journey, pouring out his grace and mercy when you confidently ask for what you need.[2]

Oh, how I wish that everyone felt free enough to ask for what they want instead of sitting in fear, stress, and isolation because they won't disclose their need. And I believe God feels the same way about his children.

Don't waste another minute missing out on everything God is standing at the ready to do for you if you confidently present your needs to him. Believe that your requests, big or small, are significant to God and that he's more than prepared to meet them. God may not give us everything we think we want, but he always gives us what he knows we need. It's time to speak up, my friend. God is ready to listen and help you.

HOW STRESS GETS STUCK

Sedentary. I downloaded a pedometer app to begin monitoring the number of steps I was taking each day. After a week of tracking, to my surprise and dismay, I realized that my numbers fell within the sedentary range. Working from home, tending to my family, and shopping primarily online didn't have me up and moving as much as I'd assumed I was. I knew that a sedentary lifestyle could lead to all sorts of problems, but not for a moment did I think that applied to me.

Being sedentary helps keep stress trapped within the body. A body that isn't exercised produces and releases pain-killing endorphins at a much lower rate, is more prone to anxiety disorders and clinical depression, and rids the body of stress hormones, such as cortisol, at a slower, physically detrimental pace. Inactivity can cause the brain to wither because exercise triggers new brain cell growth.

Sedentary practices increase one's all-cause mortality, which means the risk of death as a result of any accident, complication, exposure, or disease.[3] They also adversely impact the risk of cancer, metabolic disorders such as diabetes and hypertension, cardiovascular disease mortality, musculoskeletal disorders such as osteoporosis, and cognitive impairment. A sedentary lifestyle also increases the risk of weight gain, decreased metabolism, and vein-related problems as blood flow is decreased and moved more slowly through the veins.

Being sedentary reminds me of having a kink in an IV line. Even though you have what you need within the IV bag, the obstruction decreases the flow of fluid into the body. Similarly, your body contains the feel-good endorphins that can help reduce stress, relieve pain, and improve your sense of well-being, but the lack of movement decreases the flow of them throughout your body. It also decreases your ability to remove waste and toxins more efficiently out of the body.

Having the awareness that my routine had become sedentary enabled me to make some necessary changes and intentionally move more frequently. You'd be surprised at how quickly you can shift your stress and feel better in your body.

Trapped. Did you know that the brain doesn't feel pain? It has billions of neurons and receives pain signals from elsewhere in the body, but the brain itself has no pain receptors. Your sensory receptors process input from the environment, so if you touch a hot stove, the sensory receptors in your skin send a message via nerve fibers to your spinal cord and brainstem, and then to your brain, so that the sensation of pain registers and is processed.

When physical or emotional pain is unprocessed, either because it was so overwhelming that the mind shut down in the middle of the experience or because damage to an area of the body distorts the signal or blocks it from moving through the proper pathway, the pain and stress remain trapped in your body.

Nerve dysfunction. Nerve damage caused by an accident or a sports injury can compress, stretch, crush, or cut your nerves. A nerve injury can impact the brain's ability to communicate with organs and muscles; damaged nerve fibers can send the wrong signals to pain receptors and nerve function can be altered. When your nervous system is damaged or not working properly, you can experience neuropathic pain. When there's a change or disturbance of function in one or several nerves, it's called neuropathy. Diabetes is often associated with neuropathy, but hundreds of diseases are linked to this type of pain. This ongoing sensation of pain can cause you stress, and the ongoing presence of stress can contribute to the development of neuropathy as adrenaline, cortisol, and inflammation damage nerves.

Poor posture. Do yourself a favor and give some attention to your posture right now. Prolonged sitting promotes poor posture, and poor posture can lead to tension and both physical and mental stress. Improper working postures contribute to depression, anxiety, and various forms of pain. Over time, the tissues in your neck and upper back can adapt in an attempt to support your bad posture, making it harder to sit upright when you want to, causing additional stress.

Prolonged poor posture can also lead to prolonged stress, eventually resulting in sympathetic dominance, a state in which your stress response is overreactive, leaving you feeling overworked, overwhelmed, easily startled, and unable to calm down. This can then lead to gastrointestinal issues, poor sleep, and sensitivity to light and sound.

Stuck emotions. If you have an inability to communicate or express your emotions or find it difficult to understand why you feel the way you do, you may have an emotional blockage. If you intentionally numb yourself to feelings and emotions to avoid getting hurt by them, you may be experiencing emotional detachment. This suppression may occur if you've been taught not to express your emotions or that your feelings are invalid. Either of these conditions can cause your emotions to get stuck in your body, and the unresolved emotions can cause physical symptoms of pain, muscle tension, and the stress response.

Your voice. In addition to your emotions being stuck, you might find that your words get stuck too. Whether you're attempting to protect yourself from reliving a stressful situation or you fear retaliation in one form or another, you may find yourself at a loss for words and unable to speak up for yourself when you want to. Once you've had time away from the stressor, you might say something like, "I wish I would've said . . . " or "Why didn't I say . . . ?" making the experience more frustrating because you didn't have, or seize, the opportunity to speak.

When the suppression of your voice occurs, for whatever reason, you may begin to experience other symptoms or behaviors that are trying to be expressed. Your stuck words could present as a headache in adults, or a tummy ache in children. Or it may be displayed as uncharacteristic behaviors that are a byproduct of the words you were unable to vocalize. This is because suppressed words are like pinball games. The words that don't get to be spoken bounce around on the inside of you seeking an exit. Sometimes they come to rest on the inside and turn into aches, pain, or disease. Or they bounce around outside of you hitting targets they weren't meant for and racking up more damage as they go. Giving your words a safe space to live outside of you, whether in a spoken or written format, offers a path toward healing, restores your confidence, and enables you to reclaim your voice.

HOW STRESS KEEPS YOU STUCK

There was a cyst on his eyelid completely impairing his vision. And though his eyes were healthy, and his sight was typically clear, the blocked gland was causing an obstruction that required a visit to the operating room.

The draining of the cyst happened fast, as if the body was just waiting for the opportunity to release the old blood the cyst contained. The procedure immediately restored the patient's vision and allowed the taut skin to relax and reconstruct his appearance.

Sometimes we can't see what's right in front of us, including God's goodness, mercy, grace, and peace because the stress in our lives has greatly impaired our vision. It's blocking out truth, it's creating dysfunction, and it's causing even more stress.

When we decide to live with our stress, some parts of us remain stuck behind it, impairing our sight and our ability to navigate the world clearly. What we see, hear, and experience and how we relate to God, ourselves, and others are distorted by our stress-filled perspective.

Whether you can quickly get rid of your stress or not, attempting to do so can help restore your ability to see and reconstruct you to more closely resemble Christ.

MOVE YOUR BODY

The ability to move your body freely is a privilege many take for granted. Stretching, walking, dancing, and the endless variety of ways you can move should be done intentionally, with joy, and in an effort to support, maintain, and heal your body.

Movement and exercise do not have to include punishing your body for that treat you decided to have, or because you no longer like how you look when you pass a mirror. Movement should be a practice that acknowledges the strength, power, and wisdom of your body as it carries you through your everyday life. Let's explore a few things you can do to help you look forward to moving your body while reinforcing its strength and abilities.

The first tip is to do something you enjoy. Starting and remaining consistent with a physical movement and wellness plan becomes easier when you're exercising or moving your body in ways that you enjoy.

Movement should never feel like a punishment or done with resentment, so find and stick to routines you enjoy.

Next, be sure to check in with your body and pay attention to the signs and signals your body is sending you. If you are tired or already in pain, if you're dehydrated or it's been a while since you've moved your body, check in with yourself. Make sure you aren't pushing too hard too fast and that you're treating your body with love and respect.

Then learn how to combine your practices. Consider combining music, meditation, or mindfulness practices with your movement routine. Adding these other practices can make your routine more enjoyable and can help you create a plan that you'll stick with.

You can also change where you practice. Switching up where you work out can help keep your practice fresh. Going between your home, the gym, and a variety of outdoor locations is a simple way to help yourself remain excited about moving your body.

Also remember that exercise and movement are an investment in yourself. When you pause to think about the many benefits of moving your body—from stress reduction to pain relief to moving the toxins out of your body and improving your flexibility—you remind yourself that moving can be fun and enables you to live healthier and stronger in your body.

IMPROVE YOUR POSTURE

Poor posture, including shoulders that are rounded forward, a misaligned head that's shifted in front of the spine, or a curved upper back, can lead to distress in your body. A slouched position compresses abdominal organs, restricts the diaphragm, and interferes with the function of the vagus nerve, which is responsible for relaxing tension, establishing homeostasis, and counteracting activity of the sympathetic nerves. A dysfunctional vagus nerve can worsen chronic stress and increase the likelihood of anxiety, depression, panic attacks, insomnia, digestive issues, and autoimmune disorders.

But even if your posture has been problematic for years, it's possible to make improvements. Good posture can prevent pain and injuries, reduce stress, maintain your self-esteem, and improve your mood.

You can improve your posture while sitting by making sure that your feet touch the floor. If that's not possible, you can use a footrest. Relax your shoulders and pull them back so they're not rounded. Make sure your back is fully supported, using a pillow for support if necessary.

To improve your posture while standing, stand up straight with your shoulders back. Keep your head level, pull your stomach in, and put most of your weight on the balls of your feet.

To improve your vagus nerve function for the purpose of increasing relaxation and to strengthen your vagus nerve response, take slow, deep breaths, gargle, sing, expose yourself to cold conditions, such as splashing cold water on your face or taking a cold shower, and try fasting. These practices can improve your vagal tone and increase your capacity to regulate stress responses.

Let's Relax

RELEASE

Where do you hold stress in your body? Are there areas in your body that are consistently tense or in pain?

Do you sit for long periods of time or do you lack exercise in your routine? How does stress impact your desire or ability to move?

REESTABLISH

Therefore, I urge you, brothers and sisters, in view of God's mercy, to offer your bodies as a living sacrifice, holy and pleasing to God—this is your true and proper worship. (Romans 12:1)

Do you not know that your bodies are temples of the Holy Spirit, who is in you, whom you have received from God? You are not your own. (1 Corinthians 6:19)

RECEIVE

How to move for relaxation. There are a variety of ways you can move your body for the purpose of relaxation. You may select aerobic exercise, strength training, or integrative practices such as yoga, tai chi, or qi gong. The purpose of whatever movement you choose should be to shift your internal environment, ridding your body of toxins, fueling up on beneficial endorphins, calming the mind, and grounding your spirit. And just as these integrative practices combine mental awareness with breathing and physical exercise to help you reduce stress, relax, and enhance your well-being, you can make however you choose to move serve the same purpose. Move your body in order to get your blood flowing, enhance your energy levels, improve your posture, and increase your flexibility. All of which will also help you relax.

Stretching is an intentional movement practice that engages your relaxation response, helps reduce stress, and offers another way to glorify God with your mind, body, and spirit. Stretching releases muscle tension, improves blood flow, increases flexibility and serotonin levels, and releases endorphins that reduce pain, improve your mood, and help you relax.

Your stretching practice can be modified to fit your needs. You can begin by standing, or sitting in a chair or on the floor. While you stretch, think about every single muscle movement, focus on your alignment, and have the best posture possible. Areas in your neck, shoulders, back, and legs get lots of attention during a stretching practice, so remember to include the often neglected muscles, including those in your face and feet. Stretching facial muscles can improve their tone, while stretching feet muscles can help improve stability and decrease your risk of injury.

How to manipulate soft tissue for relaxation. Massage therapy, the manual treatment of soft body tissues to relieve pain, reduce stress, and enhance health and well-being, is one of the most familiar soft tissue manipulation practices. Massage increases the temperature of the soft tissues, such as muscles, tendons, ligaments, and connective tissue, which causes them to relax and loosen. It also lowers heart rate and releases endorphins.

Massage therapy is typically performed by a licensed massage therapist; however, you can also perform self-massage by using your hands or other tools to manipulate your own muscles.

Cupping is another form of soft tissue manipulation that involves placing cups on the skin and removing the air from the cups to create suction in order to increase blood and lymph flow. Some believe that cupping also helps to rid the body of toxins, helps relax tight or tense muscles, and alleviates pain.

Cupping can be done by a trained professional; however, there are home kits that can also provide relief. Be sure to do your research and consult with a professional before trying this practice at home.

Gua sha uses pressure and a smooth-edged tool to scrape along the skin for the purpose of breaking down scar tissue, promoting lymphatic drainage, improving circulation, relieving tension, decreasing inflammation, and ultimately helping the body to relax.

You'll need a gua sha stone, which is typically made of jade or rose quartz, to practice. You then apply even strokes against your skin in the direction of lymphatic flow. An easy, gentle stroke against your skin is usually enough to stimulate lymphatic flow and drainage.

PRAYER

Dear God, thank you for the vessel you've given me to navigate this world. Help me to care for it, moving my body to the best of my ability and maintaining strength throughout my lifetime. Help me to enjoy and celebrate my capacity to exercise, viewing it as a gift and an act of service instead of a burden or waste of time. In Jesus' name, amen.

12

Realign Your Spirit

THE PATIENT HAD chronic obstructive pulmonary disease, also known as COPD, and every breath was a struggle. COPD causes the airways and tiny air sacs in the lungs to lose their ability to stretch and shrink, and the walls of the airways become thick and inflamed. The airways make more mucus than usual, and the thickening and inflammation cause the airways to narrow, clogging them and blocking airflow. So this patient wheezed, coughed, and gasped for air continuously, and it was hard to watch. As a care provider, I care, no matter the length of the encounter or the cause of the condition. So as a student, hearing that there was nothing that could be done other than to keep her as comfortable as possible made me feel hopeless.

It is the Lord who breathed his breath into our lungs. It is his power and grace that sustain us. Sometimes our lives are so clogged and congested by stress that even when we wait in his presence, attempting to breathe him in, it can feel like a struggle, choking and drowning in the mess we're in. And we can't seem to understand why we're not experiencing his peace. We wonder if he hears us and if he still cares, unable to recognize that the air we breathe, his holy presence, has always been present, while we're too clogged up to fully receive him.

Spiritual stress can amplify physical suffering and negatively affect quality of life. Symptoms of spiritual distress can appear in all areas of your life. Spiritually, one may experience a crisis of faith, which can include emotional suffering, loss of community, feelings of grief or despair, painful questioning and confusion, and a sense of disconnection from God. Physically, spiritual stress may show up as difficulty sleeping or intractable pain, pain that's difficult to manage and is unaffected by drug administration or standard medical care. Mentally, spiritual stress may show up as hopelessness, anxiety, or depression. And socially, one may experience breakdowns in relationships. You and your stress are not hopeless, however. You still have time to clear the stress out of the spaces in your life so you can hear, see, and experience God with greater clarity.

REATTACHING

He arrived at the operating room straight from the construction site where he had lost part of his finger in an accident. The surgeon worked quickly, using magnification and smaller-than-normal instruments in an effort to repair what had been damaged.

When a traumatic accident occurs and someone loses a limb or appendage, there's a window of opportunity to reattach what has been severed. The reattachment process requires blood vessels, tendons, nerves, and skin to be realigned and meticulously stitched back together before circulation and sensation are lost for good.

Sometimes these replantation surgeries are successful and what was cut off survives. Yet there can still be residual pain, stiffness, numbness, temperature sensitivity, and loss of use of the injured part.

Can I tell you how happy I am that it's not like that with God? You can instantly realign with him at any time, no matter how long you've been cut off from his presence. God is a masterful surgeon, able to reattach you to the body, restore circulation, and remove any pain or resemblance of injury. And there is no loss of use. Isaiah 44:22 says, "I have swept away your offenses like a cloud, your sins like the morning mist. Return to me, for I have redeemed you." God has redeemed you and can use you as you are, stitching together all that you've been through for your good and his glory.

SPIRITUAL POSITIONING

In the operating room, the devices used to make patients more comfortable and to prevent injuries during surgeries are called positioners. Being out of alignment, for even short periods of time, can cause significant problems to your skin, joints, nerves, and surrounding tissues.

One can develop pressure wounds, experience poor circulation, and have problems with mobility if they're not properly positioned. And the same holds true for our spiritual positioning as well.

In Matthew 6:33 (AMP) we are told, "But first and most importantly seek (aim at, strive after) His kingdom and His righteousness [His way of doing and being right—the attitude and character of God], and all these things will be given to you also."

This means that our position is to always seek God's kingdom, his righteousness, and his way of doing things first—before we go to our best friend, social media, our coworkers, etc. We are to seek God's perspective and way, aligning our minds and thoughts with his attitude and character. And when we do, he will take the responsibility of meeting your needs.

In Proverbs 3:5 we are told to "Trust in the LORD with all your heart and lean not on your own understanding." This means that we can put our full weight on the Lord, entirely and without exception, believing in his reliability and strength. We don't have to understand a thing because more likely than not, our own understanding won't sustain us anyway.

And in 1 Thessalonians 5:16-18 we are told to "Rejoice always, pray continually, give thanks in all circumstances; for this is God's will for you in Christ Jesus." This means that our position is to be in constant communication with God, rejoicing, praying, and giving thanks, whether or not we like or understand what's going on. We can do this because we know that no matter what we're up against, God is working things out in our lives.

This is how we are to position our lives, because in doing so we endure fewer wounds, experience less stress, and are ready and able to move when God directs us to, unhindered by damaging mobility issues that result from being out of position.

You see, when we are in the place where God told us to be, we spend less time waiting for him to correct us and move us into the position he told us to be in. In this position, we can relax knowing that God has got us taken care of no matter what we are faced with.

STANDARD ATTIRE

Anyone preparing to touch the patient during a surgical operation must scrub in, cleaning their fingers, fingernails, palms, the back sides of their hands, and both forearms with a brush. Then they must keep both hands raised in the air so that the water drips off at the elbow. They must back into the OR suite, being sure they don't touch anything. Then they are handed a sterile towel to dry off before carefully putting on a sterile gown and placing each hand into sterile gloves. This attire protects the patient, as well as the member of the surgical team who's wearing it.

We understand that blood is easy to see, but the potential for other harmful substances to affect or infect everyone involved is also there. So we protect against what we can and cannot see, remaining covered from head to toe for the duration of the surgery. If we take this much care in the operating room, how much more important is it to follow the instruction we find in Ephesians 6:11-12, which tells us to "Put on the full armor of God, so that you can take your stand against the devil's schemes. For our struggle is not against flesh and blood, but against the rulers, against the authorities, against the powers of this dark world and against the spiritual forces of evil in the heavenly realms."

It's critical that we protect ourselves against what can only be seen in the spiritual realm, because those things still affect the physical realm. We need to be strengthened by the Lord and protected by his armor because our human strength isn't enough to fight against the spiritual forces of evil. We have to fight the spiritual with the spiritual. In the operating room, we understand that putting on our surgical attire doesn't eliminate the presence of various viruses and contaminants. It does however promote safety and stop us from becoming drenched in blood, dirt, and infectious particles. So as believers, we must also understand that standing in the full armor of God doesn't stop spiritual forces or spiritual warfare from taking place. But it does stop it from defeating us.

WAKE UP

When a patient is waking up from an operation, their name is called repeatedly. They're asked if they know who they are and where they are, and sometimes they're reminded to breathe as they're no longer connected to the ventilator that was previously doing this work for them. All of this effort is made to orient them and bring them back into awareness of what has just taken place.

I want you to recognize that God is constantly operating on you, showing you the things that need to be cut out of your life, where you need to place stents to keep his presence and truth flowing, and reconstructing you to resemble him more and more each day. And in the process, he's calling your name, attempting to wake you up and re-orient you to who you currently are and the new things he's doing in your life. Isaiah 43:18-19 reminds us, "Forget the former things; do not dwell on the past. See, I am doing a new thing! Now it springs up; do you not perceive it?"

My friend, it profits you nothing to become acutely aware of what your relaxation response is and how your body functions, and yet have little or no knowledge of, or relationship with, God. You don't want to work on yourself in order to remain the same or become a better version of the person you want to be or are comfortable with. No, this work is designed to wake you up and lead you into repentance when you expose aspects of your mind, body, spirit, and life that are antithetical to God.

It's time to breathe, worship him who called you out of darkness into his wonderful light, and remember who you are. You are a child of God. You are healed. You are delivered. You are set free. You are a new creation. You are seen, saved, safe, and loved. And you must exist with this constant awareness. Doing so realigns your spirit, keeping you in unison with God, undistracted by the things of this world.

BECOMING SPIRITUALLY GROUNDED

Some operations require a surgeon to use electrocauterization. This method uses a penlike instrument and electricity to apply heat to the tissue being operated on, either to stop the bleeding or remove tissue. When this is in use, a grounding pad is placed on the patient, usually on the thigh, to protect the patient from the harmful effects of electricity by safely returning the electrical current back to the generator it's plugged into.

You see, when you're grounded and plugged into your Lord and Savior, his presence protects you from the constant currents of chaos and confusion circulating all around you. You can even feel the heat and not despair knowing that he holds the power and is keeping you safe.

You also know that when he is the one bringing the heat, cauterizing stressful and unbeneficial things from your life, stopping the bleeding in the areas where you've been wounded, and sealing off paths he doesn't want you to take, you are indeed safe, grounded in him, and able to allow him to do whatever work is necessary with peace of mind.

Occasionally, someone will forget to plug the grounding pad into the generator, and you know what? The cautery pen won't work. So as you attempt to cut stress out of your life and dive deeper into relaxation, know that your efforts are in vain if you're not plugged into the power Source. Without grounding yourself in the Lord and his truth, you simply won't be as effective at excising stress, mending wounds, or sealing yourself off from the aspects of life that aren't beneficial for you. And when you are spiritually grounded, every little thing, comment, or side eye won't disturb you. Instead of feeling attacked, you'll feel the need to pray. Instead of being offended, you'll show up to serve and still have a sincere smile on your face. Instead of remaining stuck in your stress and those self-imposed limitations, you'll understand and embody that absolutely nothing is impossible with God. And you'll get up right now to go put your grounding pad on, grounding yourself in God, because you understand that there's no more time to waste.

Let's Relax

RELEASE

Are you willing to uncover the sources of your pain and stress? Why or why not?

Are you upset with God about something that has taken place in your life? Why?

How have you attempted to carry or get rid of your stress without God?

REESTABLISH

Create in me a pure heart, O God, and renew a steadfast spirit within me. (Psalm 51:10)

I will give them an undivided heart and put a new spirit in them;
I will remove from them their heart of stone and give them a heart of flesh. (Ezekiel 11:19)

RECEIVE

How to practice solitude for relaxation. Solitude gives you space to exist without external expectations. Solitude can be a restorative practice that helps you relax, think, and listen to yourself and God more closely. It can also help to increase creativity, self-awareness, spirituality, and healing.

You can practice solitude at home or out in nature. Simply schedule time to be alone, find a calm, quiet space, and then do something just for you. You can pray, stretch, meditate, read, write, sit still, or a combination of all these things.

Another way to practice solitude is by participating in a digital detox. With the abundant use of technology, there's an increase in technostress in which one feels tension, anxiety, or distress because they're overwhelmed by technology, their interpersonal online connections, or are experiencing information overload. Being connected 24-7 can become burdensome and negatively affect one's personal and professional well-being.

During a digital detox, all technology is turned off, including smartphones, computers, TVs, social media, and other digital devices. Digital detoxing improves mental health, decreases stress, sharpens concentration, and enhances relationships.

Another way to practice solitude is by participating in a silent retreat. Silent retreats enable you to voluntarily remain silent, pause external distractions, become introspective, and create space to be fully present in your life and with God. In silence, you can listen to your inner longings and inner wisdom to receive spiritual guidance without the constant noise of the external world.

How to use guided imagery for relaxation. Guided imagery is a relaxation technique that uses the power of your imagination to visualize a positive and peaceful setting to reduce stress and encourage a relaxed state. Just as your brain doesn't distinguish between an actively stressful situation or one that you're imagining can happen, your brain doesn't distinguish between you looking at a relaxing scene that you're present in or one that you're solely imagining.

Examples of guided imagery techniques include the following:

- Imagining yourself relaxing in the most peaceful and serene location
- Imagining your white blood cells fighting off illness
- Imagining being in the presence of God and hearing him say to you well done, good and faithful servant

Just imagine what could happen, and the life you would live, if you began to visualize, imagine, and embody every wonderful truth God says and believes about you. Second Corinthians 4:18 says, "So we fix our eyes not on what is seen, but on what is unseen, since what is seen is temporary, but what is unseen is eternal." The stresses and trials in your life should not overshadow your peace and joy if you're maintaining your focus on the eternal realities that'll last forever. Your ability to see what cannot be seen may take a bit of imagination, but doing so can change your current realities by amplifying the eternal ones.

How to utilize prayer for relaxation. First Thessalonians 5:17 tells us to "pray continually," and doing so comes with spiritual, mental, and physical benefits. Prayer has a calming effect on your nervous system, reducing stress, lowering blood pressure, reducing feelings of isolation, anxiety, and fear, lowering reactivity to negative events, and eliciting the relaxation response.

Prayers can be silent or spoken, specific requests or have no special outcomes in mind, so there isn't one set way to pray. Prayer has been found to be the most widely used complementary medical and healing practice there is.

Devotional prayer, which includes prayers that are in praise of God and prayers for the well-being of others, seem to be most effective in lowering anxiety.[1]

Now let's exercise our faith and pray. Dear God, thank you for the opportunity to restore my relationship with you, to release every care, fear, stress, and anxious thought into your hands. Guide me as I seek to eliminate stress from my life so that I can experience the depths of relaxation and peace available to me. In Jesus' name, amen.

Praise and worship. In addition to prayer, praise and worship also benefit our ability to relax. Hebrews 13:15 says, "Through Jesus, therefore, let us continually offer to God a sacrifice of praise—the fruit of lips that openly profess his name." While the devil was trying to tempt Jesus to worship him, "Jesus answered, 'It is written:

"Worship the Lord your God and serve him only"'" (Luke 4:8). So even though we have the ability to worship other people and other things, we are wired to solely worship God. Worshiping anything or anyone other than him will further perpetuate the disconnection of your relationships, distortion of your thoughts, and disruption of your spiritual and emotional well-being. Praise, however, which is about God, and worship, which is to God, change the physical structure and enhance the function of your brain, decrease activation of the stress response, bear spiritual, mental, and physical fruit, and create an atmosphere that encourages activation of the relaxation response.

How to meditate for relaxation. Meditation has been shown to improve mental health by reducing stress and anxiety, increasing emotional well-being, improving focus and concentration, and promoting better sleep. Regular meditation practice can also lead to changes in brain function and structure that support better mental health.

Meditation has various benefits for your physical health as well, such as reducing inflammation, lowering blood pressure, improving sleep quality, and reducing symptoms of chronic pain. It may also help boost the immune system and promote overall well-being.

Meditation can help improve your spiritual health by allowing you to foster a deeper connection with God and your own spirit and help you gain a deeper understanding of your beliefs and values. It can also increase feelings of gratitude, compassion, and forgiveness.

Christian meditation is not an attempt to empty the mind. It's an intentional attempt to become aware of and reflect on the revelations of God. In Colossians 3:2 we're reminded to set our minds on things above, and in Joshua 1:8 we're told to meditate on the book of instruction day and night, rolling it over in our minds so that the Word of God becomes deeply rooted into our souls. This type of meditation cultivates our faith, trust, and relationship with God.

You can get creative with your meditation practice, incorporating multiple meditation styles such as concentrative, guided, or walking.

The following steps will offer you a few ideas to help you launch, or continue, your concentrative meditation practice:

1. Choose a quiet place to sit.
2. Sit with your back straight and relax your shoulders.
3. Close your eyes and take a few deep breaths.
4. Focus your attention on your breath, either the sensation of air moving in and out of your nostrils or the rising and falling of your chest.
5. Center your thoughts on a particular Scripture, song, or story from the Bible that encourages you and makes you feel at peace, that applies to your day or an area of your life in which you want God's guidance.
6. If your mind starts to wander, gently bring it back to your breath.
7. Start with just a few minutes a day and gradually increase the time as you become more comfortable with your meditation practice.

If you'd prefer to move while you meditate, here are a few ideas for a walking meditation practice.

Walking meditation has many benefits, including reducing stress and anxiety, improving focus and concentration, and increasing feelings of calm and relaxation.

To use walking as a meditation, find a quiet and peaceful place where you can walk uninterrupted for ten to fifteen minutes. As you walk, focus on your breath and the sensation of your feet hitting the ground. If your mind starts to wander, gently bring your attention back to your breath and your steps.

I often use music in conjunction with my walking meditation, listening to instrumental hymns or nature sounds to help create a peaceful atmosphere and enhance my focus. Remember, the goal is to use music as a tool to enhance your meditation practice, not to distract from it.

The ideal length of a meditation session can vary, depending upon your personal preference and your schedule. However, starting with five to ten minutes per day and gradually increasing the duration can be a good approach for beginners. Ultimately, it's important to find a duration that works best for you and allows you to cultivate relaxation.

PRAYER

Lord, it is your breath that sustains us, your Spirit that dwells within us, your mind that has created us and knit us together in our mothers' wombs. Thank you for the ability to reconcile our relationship with you, to exist in your presence, and to commune with you once again. For this we are immensely grateful. Help us to live in constant awareness of your presence, reflecting and exhibiting you for the world to see. In Jesus' name, amen.

13

Revive Your Relationships

TIME AND TIME AGAIN the Bible illustrates that God created humans to be in community with one another. Mark 12:31 teaches us that after our wholehearted love for God, there is no greater commandment than to love your neighbor as yourself. And Philippians 2:2 describes the joy that comes from unity among God's people who have the same love and are one in spirit and of one mind. So it is imperative that we nurture our relationships, cultivating love, unity, and forgiveness with others, which is pleasing to God. Yet this isn't always a simple, amenable task. Relationships, and the interactions we have with other humans, can take work, cause us stress, test every aspect of our faith, and force us to respond to God's call for us to embrace the suffering of doing life with other imperfect human beings. This call requires us to stop trying to run away from relationships in an attempt to avoid inevitable stress and suffering, and to enter into relationships not concerned about if or how we will be wounded, trusting that God is in control of it all. As we strive to partner with God and be at peace with his desire for us to dwell in community and cultivate relationships, it's important to understand how social and relational stress impact our lives.

SOCIAL STRESS

Social stress includes social situations and behaviors that cause physical or psychological strain, feelings of discomfort or anxiety, or threats to one's relationships, sense of belonging, or esteem. Socially stressful events can include social isolation, the loss of a loved one, bullying, psychological abuse, a difficult marriage or partnership, divorce, retirement, socioeconomic disadvantage, unemployment, bad traffic, sudden injury, sexual assault, and discrimination. Social stress doesn't necessarily happen because of a specific event. Sometimes when one perceives that they don't have the resources to cope with a specific social situation, the mere thought that an event may occur is enough to trigger social stress. Typically, social stress is the most frequent type of stressor one experiences, as well as the one experienced most intensely.[1]

Social stress impacts one's mental, physical, and spiritual health. It increases the risk of developing negative mental health outcomes including depression, anxiety, sleeping problems, and substance use problems. Social stress is associated with higher rates of illness, worse health outcomes, and increased mortality rates. And because we are designed for connection and relationship, social stress also impacts our spiritual health. In fact, it can arise from our spiritual neglect and disobedience. We are to love our neighbors as ourselves (Galatians 5:14); be kind, tenderhearted, and forgiving of one another (Ephesians 4:32); and to encourage one another and meet together (Hebrews 10:24-25). These practices are a means provided by God to help us, and not doing them limits God's work in our lives and disrupts our spiritual wellbeing. We need to be extended love, encouragement, support, kindness, and forgiveness from those around us in our everyday lives; when this is lacking, we can fall into spiritual distress and disconnection.

LONELINESS AND SOCIAL ISOLATION

Loneliness had reached epidemic levels prior to the global pandemic that led to an even greater increase in social isolation and loneliness. Loneliness is the feeling of being alone or disconnected from others. People experiencing loneliness usually feel like they don't have close or meaningful relationships or a true sense of belonging. So even someone with many friends can feel lonely if there is a difference between their actual and desired level of connection. Social isolation is a lack of relationships with others, and little to no social contact or support. And even if one doesn't feel lonely, they are still at risk of the detrimental effects of social isolation.

Whether one withdraws socially because of social stress, anxiety, or depression, or becomes socially stressed, anxious, or depressed because they're lonely or isolated, the consequences are significant. Social isolation is associated with a 50 percent increased risk of dementia, and a 26 percent increased risk of premature death. Social isolation and loneliness increase the likelihood of heart disease, stroke, diabetes, anxiety, depression, addiction, self-harm, suicidal tendencies, earlier death, and reduced quality of life.

TOXIC RELATIONSHIPS

Toxic relationships have unhealthy dynamics that cause you distress or harm. They make you feel misunderstood, unsupported, disrespected, demeaned, or attacked; they can be described with words such as insecurity, dishonesty, jealousy, negativity, hostility, abuse of power, distrust, criticism, dependency, intimidation, demeaning comments; and they can have physical, emotional, or sexual violence. It's important to note that not all these indicators have to be present for a toxic relationship to exist. And being ill-equipped to handle or remove yourself from these dynamics can heighten one's social stress.

Toxic relationships can make you feel bad about yourself, drain you of your energy, and stunt your ability to grow and thrive. Unfortunately, it can be difficult for a person to stand up for or separate themselves from a toxic person and relationship, causing them to feel stuck in cycles of abuse and toxicity that negatively impact their mental, physical, emotional, and spiritual health.

Toxic relationships can lead to excessive rumination, which is your mind's way of alerting you that there's an emotional injury in need of healing. Rumination involves excessive or repetitive thinking or dwelling on the same event, negative feelings or experiences, and distress. Excessively ruminating over interactions, conversations, and experiences can trigger the stress response, negative emotions, and the development of depression or anxiety, and can worsen existing conditions.

Co-rumination can also occur when you repeatedly discuss or rehash problems with others without coming up with a solution. This behavior can keep you stuck and lead to symptoms of anxiety and depression. The challenge arises from the desire to vent and think things through with someone else, because doing so can be a beneficial process. Talking things out can feel good, offer you a sense of relief, and make you believe you're doing something productive, but if you never pause to consider the ways you can change or improve whatever you're discussing, you'll remain stuck in cycles of rumination, hindering your ability to heal and move forward.

WHEN YOU DON'T FEEL HEARD BY YOUR CARE PROVIDER

If you feel that your care provider is not listening to you, acting dismissive, and making you feel unheard, this is another form of social stress that can negatively impact your health and healing. When those you turn to for support don't seem to be paying attention, seem hurried, and don't display to you that they care, this can lead to distrust of your care providers and impact your willingness to partner with those who are meant to support you. This can also lead to stressful interactions, or for some, a lack of motivation to schedule and attend care visits. This can disrupt your prevention and wellness routine, causing you to miss opportunities to heal minor issues before they become chronic problems and result in detrimental consequences.

THE NECESSITY OF RELATIONSHIPS

She hadn't seen or talked to her family in months, but she refused to participate in the delivery of her baby until the staff could get them on the phone. She crossed her legs, would not push, and seemingly willed her baby to stay inside. But the inevitable was going to happen one way or another. She wrote down some numbers and the nurse proceeded to dial as quickly as she could until someone finally picked up. I was a student at the time, and as I stood next to her, I did what I always did: prayed.

The nurse attempted to explain to someone on the other end of the phone why she was calling. Then she extended her arm past me toward the young woman. The nurse held the phone to the patient's ear, and as the young woman began to speak, tears streamed down her face. I don't know the extent of what had taken place, what caused her not to speak to her loved ones or have anyone other than hospital staff and a prayerful student by her side, but there we were, witnessing someone who refused to move forward in her life-changing situation without attempting to reconnect with those who, up until that point in her life, mattered most.

After the call, she was ready, and she focused all her attention on birthing her baby. She needed that mending to occur, and she risked her safety to ensure that it would happen.

Relationships and who one considers family will vary from one person to the next. Generally, however, relationships foster a sense of connectedness and are formed by ongoing interactions and emotional bonds.

Mutually beneficial relationships include space to be heard, to share your feelings and experiences and have them acknowledged, the presence of emotional support, and the ability to live free from threat, criticism, accusation, judgment, and blame. They also need regular communication to help maintain stability and build trust. Each person takes a proactive interest in the other, in mutually beneficial relationships, so they can work together to keep their individual and collective goals moving forward. Healthy, meaningful relationships are a vital component of our overall health, as well as providing social support.

CULTIVATING RELATIONSHIPS

Relationships need time and attention in order to thrive. They also require you to continuously develop life and relational skills. Here are some tips for cultivating meaningful relationships in your life.

Forgive. Every relationship will face challenges and hurtful moments that call for forgiveness. Holding on to the memories and replaying them again and again causes you to repeatedly experience the same distress. It also creates space to allow the pain and anger to take root and sprout bitterness and resentment.

Ephesians 4:32 says, "Be kind and compassionate to one another, forgiving each other, just as in Christ God forgave you." This indicates that things will happen that require you to forgive, and that you'll need to actively practice forgiveness. When you choose to forgive, you allow yourself to experience greater peace of mind, less stress, anxiety, hostility, and symptoms of depression, lowered blood pressure, and healthier relationships.

Show compassion. Showing compassion means that you're sensitive to and show concern for the suffering and misfortune of others. A nonjudgmental display of compassion creates space to communicate and create a stronger relational bond.

Showing compassion doesn't mean that you absorb the emotion or responsibility of alleviating others' suffering. It means you extend a helping hand, show kindness, and ensure that others don't feel alone in what they're going through.

Offer acceptance. When you offer acceptance, you try to understand where another person is coming from without making any effort to attempt to change them. You acknowledge their feelings, thoughts, opinions, strengths, and weaknesses, understanding that change, if necessary, takes time, and you let go of your desire to be the change agent.

Show appreciation. Showing appreciation can strengthen relationships, as it boosts positive feelings in both the giver and the recipient. Whether you share a simple thank you, give a compliment, write a note of appreciation, or use another gesture to exhibit your gratitude, expressing your appreciation is a simple way to cultivate your relationships.

Spend time with others. Spending intentional time, fully present and engaged, with those you care about is a truly meaningful way to cultivate your relationships. When you designate time to spend together, the nurturing and support of one another can deepen your connection.

Spend time alone. Spending time by yourself can combat the stress of social overload and feelings of overstimulation. Being in tune with yourself enough to know when you need some alone time is critical to maintaining healthy relationships. Taking the time necessary to physically, mentally, spiritually, and emotionally recharge is beneficial to you and others.

Communicate effectively. Effective communication can help you share your thoughts, feelings, and opinions while developing mutual respect for each other. It can also help you avoid misunderstandings that can lead to hurt, confusion, anger, or resentment. Effective communication helps you create a safe space for sharing about the stresses in your life, how you want to change them, and the support you need to make that happen.

BUILDING YOUR SUPPORT TEAM

My colleague's surgery was scheduled for the following week. As I stood at the front desk, she presented her list, requesting who she wanted to care for her throughout the preoperative, surgical, and postoperative procedures.

Her surgeon of choice had long been established, and she now wanted to ensure that the nurses, surgical techs, and anesthesiologists whom she trusted would be present with her.

Barring no emergencies, this would be her team, the people who made her feel seen, heard, and safe, which were all critical to both her operation and her healing.

Because she worked alongside them, she was well aware of their capabilities and the type and level of care she would receive. She advocated on her own behalf, made her requests known, and improved her ability to show up confidently for her procedure.

In the same way, you get to choose who supports you and surround yourself with those who make you feel seen, heard, and safe. The people in your life, including your family, friends, and health care providers, and the relationships you cultivate with them, are vital to your healing and relaxation.

Thankfully, I'm a nurse, a part of the profession that gets ranked the most trusted year after year in the United States. Nurses are believed to be a healing presence to their patients through the physical, emotional, spiritual, and interpersonal care they provide. The intention to be consciously present, coupled with compassionate care, then increases the healing potential of those being cared for.

Because you're a part of my community, you get a sampling of this experience through our interactions. And you can continue to surround yourself with others who will offer you a healing presence and increase your healing potential—those who are consciously and compassionately supporting, believing, and championing your healing and your relaxation.

FAMILY AND FRIENDS

The support of family and friends can significantly reduce your stress and influence better health outcomes over the course of your life. To help you ensure that the support is mutually beneficial, here are some ways to expand your awareness of the vital impact your family and friends have on your health and well-being.

It's important to feel comfortable communicating your love, appreciation, fears, and stressors to the friends and family members you'd like to support you. Ensuring that they're aware that your relationship is meaningful, of what your struggles are, and of how you can be there for one another is critical to the health and longevity of your mutually beneficial support.

It's important that you actively work to build trust with others, allowing yourself to be vulnerable and sharing your thoughts, feelings, and stresses without the fear of judgment, abandonment, or disloyalty. Effective communication is necessary as you build trust, even if this includes sharing uncomfortable feelings because in doing so, you create space for others to do the same.

Listening to those you love with an open mind and your undivided attention is a significant way to show them that you care. This can help facilitate better communication, increase trust, and make supporting one another more effective. It can also help you effectively handle conflict.

The ability to manage conflict ensures that when difficulties arise you don't avoid challenges, or act as if they aren't happening, and you come through them stronger, and with mutual respect. Conflict management includes open communication, problem-solving skills, and a commitment to arrive at a solution. These are skills that can be learned and practiced in order to foster and sustain healthy relationships. Forgiveness may be necessary when conflict arises, as well as the willingness to invite outside support from a therapist or counselor into the relationship in order to amicably resolve any conflict.

ASK FOR HELP

Sometimes we're so used to our routines that we believe it's easier to continue doing them on our own. But this doesn't give us much help or relief from those tasks. You may require a mindset shift to understand that in order for progress to be made, you must share with others what you need help with.

Delegation is a skill that can be learned and practiced. And asking for help is a gift you give to yourself and others. Asking for help isn't a sign of weakness. It displays your self-awareness and strength.

UNDERSTANDING

It's important to surround yourself with people who won't idly sit by and watch you drown without ever offering to help you out. For example, when people are grieving, no one tends to ask the griever what they need because there's this general understanding that they need everything. Nor are they expected to pinpoint the specifics of what needs to be done in the midst of their grief. Others simply step in, cooking, cleaning, and caring for whatever presents itself.

We must exhibit this type of help even when grief isn't present.

Sometimes people aren't taught how to ask for help, have given up on asking for help, or need help with so many things that they can't pinpoint their ask. We need to get in the habit of showing up for others, seeking out ways to help and relieve their stress, and become open to this practice being reciprocated. This is how we increase one another's ability to relax and feel supported.

Whether you are the strong friend, or you're the one checking on your strong friends, understand that everyone's life experience and awareness will be different. Therefore, communication, compassion, and crisis relief will look different for each relationship and should be allowed the space for us to learn and grow in them together.

Let's Relax

RELEASE

Who do you need to forgive and why?

What experiences have you had with others that you believe you're still suffering from?

REESTABLISH

> Two are better than one, because they have a good return for their labor: If either of them falls down, one can help the other up. But pity anyone who falls and has no one to help them up. (Ecclesiastes 4:9-10)

> Be kind and compassionate to one another, forgiving each other, just as in Christ God forgave you. (Ephesians 4:32)

> Therefore encourage one another and build each other up, just as in fact you are doing. (1 Thessalonians 5:11)

RECEIVE

How to use social support for relaxation. Having social support means that you have a network of friends, family, and people in your life that you can turn to for care and comfort in times of crisis or need.

These are the people who enhance your quality of life and create a buffer against stress and challenging life experiences.

The types of social support one can receive include emotional, feeling loved and cared for and being shown empathy and affection; physical, in the form of food, money, or labor; informational, which involves being provided with helpful information; and esteem, in the form of words of encouragement and confidence in one's ability to face and overcome difficulties.

So how does social support help you engage your relaxation response? Healthy relationships encourage you to drop your guard, relax, and trigger your body to release hormones such as oxytocin, which helps build bonds with others; dopamine, which helps us to feel satisfied; and serotonin, which helps regulate mood and increase feelings of joy and happiness.

How to practice gratitude for relaxation. First Thessalonians 5:18 says to "give thanks in all circumstances; for this is God's will for you in Christ Jesus." So it should come as no surprise that as we obey this directive, which is the will of God, we also reap several benefits.

Gratitude, the thankful appreciation for what you receive, whether tangible or intangible, acknowledges the good in your life and helps you connect with God and others. Gratitude helps to relieve stress, reduce anxiety and depression, and improve mood, sleep, and immunity. It also improves heart health.

Practicing gratitude is both a reminder and, many times, spiritual warfare. Gratitude is an awareness that your life is currently good, as you're on your way toward new goals. Gratitude is a battle cry acknowledging that you're not missing out on anything, so there's no need to compare yourself or your situation to anyone else's. Gratitude declares that you're safe, never left out or behind, and not lacking anything. It's how you fight back against mental weeds that can sprout up, overgrow, and block out the truth.

In order to maximize your gratitude practice, you may need to redirect your thoughts. If something is causing stressful feelings to arise, take a deep breath, step back from the situation, and shift your focus to what you're grateful for.

Write down what you're grateful for, which you can do anytime throughout your day. You can take notes on paper or digitally and keep track of grateful moments. You can also have an intentional practice, either at the beginning or the end of your day, when you write down and reflect upon everything that you're grateful for.

Taking the time to tell someone that you're grateful for them or something they did to make your life better not only gives you the opportunity to express your gratitude, but it creates space for the recipient to experience a moment of gratitude as well.

One simple way to practice gratitude and activate your relaxation response is to start a gratitude jar. Sometime throughout your day, write down what you are grateful for and place your answers in the jar. On days when you need a reminder or you simply want to praise God for all of your blessings, you can open your jar and read what you've written.

PRAYER

Lord, how blessed we are to be in relationship with you. To be able to call upon your name and get to know you in a deeper way each day. Help us to mend our earthly relationships. To love, forgive, and unite in community with others for your glory. Help us to steward our relationships well, making your love visible for all the world to see. In Jesus' name, amen.

14

Discharge Instructions

As *RADICAL RELAXATION* CONCLUDES, I want you to know that it's been my honor to share this time and these words with you. I know that talking about stress isn't easy, and it brings up some of the most difficult aspects of our lives. So please know that I delivered this to you with empathy, compassion, and prayer. And now it's time for me to transfer care into your very capable hands.

You've been equipped with the information, tools, and resources you need to continue releasing your stress and recovering your relaxation. To ensure that your progress continues after you've completed this book, and to help you make relaxing an essential element of your lifestyle, I'd like to leave you with this prayer: "May the Lord direct your hearts into God's love and Christ's perseverance" (2 Thessalonians 3:5). And these discharge instructions:

Recover. Remember that recovering from the impacts of stress takes time, and you'll need to be patient as you figure out all of the various sources of stress in your life. Recovery is highly personal, and it may be necessary to utilize all the resources available to you. Sometimes the recovery process is painful. This is not something to shy away from. Facing the pain, feeling it, and finding your way through it is an essential part of your healing.

Stay committed. It's important to be patient with yourself as you begin to implement new relaxation strategies into your life. It may take multiple attempts and approaches for you to find what works for you, so remember that minor changes can yield major results if you stay committed to your relaxation practice.

Assess your readiness. Take your time returning to the places, relationships, and situations that previously caused you stress. Continuously look for ways to mend relationships and make them less stressful. The goal isn't to cut everyone who ever caused you any stress out of your life, but to pray, forgive, effectively communicate, and build stronger relationships in the process.

Give grace. Extending grace to yourself and others can help you stay committed to your relaxation practice. Being mindful of the conversation taking place within you and remembering to encourage and uplift yourself can make a significant difference when it comes to your ability to relax. Also, extend grace to loved ones. Everyone won't be able to help you with your new lifestyle changes, and they should not be made to feel guilty, ashamed, or uncomfortable if they are unwilling or unable to support your relaxation practice.

Find relaxation buddies. Having others to support you and keep you accountable as you implement new relaxation strategies can help you maximize your healing results. Plus, relaxing can be a fun way to interact with friends and explore new practices.

Evaluate your relaxation practice. Doing so will help you determine if the relaxation strategies you're implementing are meeting the intended outcome you desire to achieve. Asking yourself questions like: Is my relaxation practice working? How can I incorporate more relaxation into my life? Which relaxation practices do I not enjoy, or am not seeing any benefit from? This cultivates the habit of checking in with yourself, making necessary adjustments, and continuously moving closer to your goals.

Don't compare. The relaxation strategies you enjoy and the progress you make toward developing a consistent relaxation practice and healing the effects of stress are meaningful aspects of your journey. This doesn't mean that your friends or family will enjoy the same practices or make the same kind of progress as you. Stay focused on your goals and don't steal your own joy by comparing your journey to anyone else's.

Expect healing. Keeping your mind on the goal of healing, anticipating your experience of it, and expecting it to occur will help you avoid being discouraged by setbacks or giving up on your relaxation practice. If you expect healing, you will continue to work toward it, doing all that you can to reap the benefits of relaxation.

Cultivate your relationship with God. Stress attempts to alienate you from God, even though you've been delivered and set free. You get to choose to return to God again and again, communing with him, receiving rest in his presence, and experiencing the depths of relaxation knowing that he has all things under control. Drawing near to God is the most effective antidote to stress.

Honor your wholeness. You are a complete spiritual being having wildly unique human experiences. So you must remember to nurture all of the parts of your being, as the entirety of who you are is impacted by both stress and relaxation. Acknowledging that your mind, body, and spirit are interconnected will help you seek harmony personally, in your relationships with others, and with God.

Be radical. Radical has several meanings. To maximize the impact of relaxation in your life, review them whenever possible.

1. *Remove*—to cut off stress and separate yourself from its harmful effects.

2. *Redeem*—to make the conscious choice to intentionally change the fundamental nature of how you've been existing. In this case, you're changing an existence filled with stress into one filled with relaxation. You are redeeming the relaxation that's always been available to you.

3. *Revolutionize*—to make the bold, and sometimes unpopular, choice to walk in obedience to the Word of God and his intended design for your life, health, and being. Even when the world attempts to pull you in other directions, even when your friends don't seem to understand, even when the choice is counter-cultural, you remain unwavering in your decision to relax because

you know that it's in this surrendered state of reverence and obedience that your relaxation and healing potential are realized.

4. *Represent*—to advocate for, support, and represent relaxation as the way forward. This means that not only have you adopted the practice of relaxation in your own life, but you also now encourage others to do the same. You understand that this information could change the course of someone's life, so you choose to be the light of the world and the salt of the earth, illuminating and flavoring as you go for the healing of God's people and the glory of God.

5. *Resource*—originating in the root, which means that you've returned to and planted yourself in your innate state of relaxation, becoming the root that relaxation now grows from. When you're the resource, you can offer up your testimony and exhibit your transformation as inspiration for others to behold.

Relax. May you know within the depths of your being that you are fearfully and wonderfully made in the image of God, the creator and sustainer of the universe, the visionary for your presence here on earth, treating yourself with the utmost respect, recognizing that you are a temple of God, a holy dwelling place for his presence, unwilling to disturb your vessel with stress or anything antithetical to who God is. May you know that your relaxation response is a healing, life-enhancing gift and remain determined to learn how to tap into it, cultivating its power, using it to support your longevity, reflecting to the world that the kingdom of God is in your midst. May you relax without apology, understanding the atmosphere-shifting impact of your actions, becoming comfortable with your peculiarities, standing boldly in the marvelous light, ready to proclaim the good news, protect your identity in Christ, propel your healing forward, and bask in the peace of God, which passes all understanding. And may you release the stress you were never intended to carry, embracing your redemption and living in unity with God's intended design for your life—relaxed.

Acknowledgments

THIS BOOK WOULD NOT EXIST without the following people's support. I would like to acknowledge Greg. Thank you for creating the space for this work to come alive, and these words to exist in this world. I truly appreciate your ongoing encouragement and support. I love you. April, what a gift it is to do life with you. Our friendship helps me thrive. I love you and thank God for you. Ma, Dad, Granny, and Aunt, your love, support, and prayers mean the world to me. I am forever grateful for each of you and the unique ways you've shaped my life. This book wouldn't have been possible without you. To The Crew: Richmond, Solomon, Bria, and Zara. Do you know how proud and blessed I am to be your Mama? It's the honor of my lifetime. Thank you for your patience throughout this writing journey. May you continue to nurture your personal relationship with God. And may he continue to bless you abundantly.

To my fellow devotions writing team. I used to pray for a team of people who could pray for me constantly. You've been the answer to that prayer. Thank you for your continuous encouragement, prayers, and support throughout this process. You're such a blessing. Jevon, my literary agent—for seeing, hearing, and journeying with me, I am endlessly grateful. I appreciate you and the trailblazing, industry-expanding work that you're doing. Thank you. And Nilwona—for seeing space in this world for this book, giving me the opportunity to bring it to life, and your patient guidance throughout the process, thank you. My deepest gratitude to you all.

Appendix A

Simple Ways to Release Stress

Go outside
Write in a journal
Take a nap
Smile on purpose
Count your blessings
Take a bubble bath
Turn off electronics and notifications for thirty minutes
Create art
Do something special for yourself
Volunteer to do something that will help someone else
Talk to a friend who knows how to encourage and celebrate you
Read something for fun
Eat a delicious and nutritious meal
Stretch
Smell a relaxing fragrance
Go for a walk
Breathe deeply
Listen to calming music
Meditate
Pray

Appendix B

When It Might Be Time to Change Your Care Provider

REMAINING WITH A CARE PROVIDER who is not adequately partnering with you regarding your care can damage your trust in the health care system, prevent you from receiving the best care, and keep you from reaching your health care goals. It's important to understand that not all care providers are alike, nor will they all be a good fit for you. So here are six signs to help you recognize when it may be time to switch providers.

1. You should always feel that your health care provider is listening to you, so if it seems that your concerns are being dismissed, ignored, or invalidated, this may be a strong indicator that it's time to find a new provider.

2. Your provider should communicate and collaborate well. Here are some signs that indicate they are poor at this and you may need to be cared for by someone else: If they use medical jargon or terms you rarely understand without making an attempt to help you understand. If they fail to listen or inform you about your care, or seem annoyed when you ask questions about your treatment. Or if they refuse to make a referral when you ask for one or won't coordinate care with other providers to help you receive the best treatment possible.

3. If they are not open to discussing alternative diagnoses or treatment options. If you've received a diagnosis and have been

following a treatment plan but don't seem to be improving, yet your provider doesn't seem interested in exploring why this is the case or the possibility of an alternative diagnosis, this may be an indicator that you need a new provider. If your care provider does not seem interested in giving you multiple options about possible treatments for any conditions you may have, this may be another sign that it's time to move on. Yes, they will likely give you best practice options, or the options that others use most frequently. This doesn't mean that other options and treatments aren't available, right for you, or shouldn't be explored.

4. If you're failing to make progress in your treatment. Whether your provider lacks expertise to treat your specific condition or you simply feel that you're not getting the care you need, this may be a sign that it's time to switch providers. You want to receive care from someone who can get you on the path to feeling better. Not someone who will help you maintain your sickness, meaning that you may feel slightly better than upon your initial interaction and treatment options, but you never feel like you completely recover or feel better.

5. If your care provider is unprofessional, not respecting your privacy or your time, has poor hygiene, or doesn't observe medical precautions, this may warrant consideration for choosing a different care provider.

6. If your care provider makes frequent mistakes, ordering incorrect tests, misplacing medical files, or failing to follow up on test results, this behavior may be a sign to move on from their care. If this provider makes an effort to hide or lie about their mistakes, this is also a red flag.

If you decide to change care providers, know that you are under no obligation to inform your current provider that you are leaving their practice. However, if you can provide valuable feedback regarding your experience under their care, and they are receptive to the feedback, you may want to share it. Another reason you may want to tell your provider that you're leaving their practice is so that you can have a discussion about your current health condition and treatment plan before you leave. Discussing the details about how to transfer your care to your new provider, including any upcoming tests, procedures, and prescriptions, may be beneficial. Whether you decide to inform them or not, be sure to submit a request for your medical records as soon as possible.

CHOOSING YOUR NEXT CARE PROVIDER

When choosing your next care provider, it's beneficial to research them and their practice before making the switch. Websites like www.healthgrades.com and www.medicare.gov/care-compare can provide you with feedback about your prospective care provider. Talking to people you know about the care providers they use and the experiences they've had with them is another helpful way to make your decision. Then schedule an appointment to meet with your new provider. You can call their office to ask if they accept your insurance. Then write down any questions or concerns you have and bring them with you on your visit. Also be sure to bring your medical records and a list of the medications you take.

Appendix C

You're Not Alone

My Friend,

This book may have been exactly what you needed to begin releasing the stress in your life. This book may have also widened your understanding about the deeper levels of healing that need to take place in your life. Sometimes we face difficult realities that will require us to be honest about our need for help. And because this book doesn't take the place of therapy, I want to offer you resources to help you navigate what you've experienced. I'd also like to acknowledge the importance of finding a counselor or therapist who shares your beliefs and commitment to a personal relationship with Jesus, and can help you fight your battles physically, mentally, emotionally, and spiritually.

- The American Association of Christian Counselors—aacc.net
- BetterHelp—Christian-based therapy and counseling option
- Therapy for Black Girls

You can also research local Christian therapy services in your area.

Glossary

Adipose tissue—connective tissue composed of adipocytes, also known as body fat

Adrenal glands—small endocrine glands located on top of your kidneys

Adrenaline—a hormone produced and secreted by the body under stressful conditions

Amenorrhea—the abnormal absence of periods

Amygdala—the region of your brain responsible for emotional processing

Anovulation—absence of ovulation; the release of an egg from the ovaries does not occur

Autonomic nervous system—the part of the nervous system that controls involuntary processes such as breathing and the heartbeat

Blood pressure—the force of circulating blood pushing against blood vessels

Cholesterol—a waxy, fatlike substance made by the liver, found in all cells in your body

Collagen fibers—the fibers that form the extracellular framework of all tissues

Cortisol—a steroid hormone produced by the adrenal gland that helps the body regulate stress and metabolism

Cytokines—small signaling proteins that help control inflammation in your body

Diagnosis—the identification of a disease from its signs and symptoms

Enzyme—a substance produced by a living organism that acts as a biological catalyst, accelerating chemical reactions

Epinephrine—also known as adrenaline, a hormone and neurotransmitter secreted by the adrenal glands in response to stress

Epithelial cells—one of the most abundant types of cells covering internal and external surfaces in your body

Epithelium—thin, continuous, protective layer of compactly packed epithelial cells

Equilibrium—a state of physical balance

Free radicals—a highly reactive and unstable molecule capable of independent existence that has at least one unpaired valence electron

Granulation tissue—connective tissue and microscopic blood vessels that fill in a wound

Hemostasis—stopping the flow of blood from a blood vessel

Histamine—a compound released by cells in response to injury, and in inflammatory and allergic reactions

Homeostasis—a self-regulating process of maintaining internal stability while adjusting to changing external conditions

Immunoprotective cells—cells that respond to wounds, viral infections, and cancer to promote healing and eliminate infection and disease

Inflammation—a natural reaction in which white blood cells protect against infection and injury

Inflammatory phase—the body's natural response to injury, the period when tissue remodeling takes place

Integumentary—the outer protective layer, the physical barrier between the internal and external environment, the body's first line of defense

Laparoscopy—a surgical procedure using small incisions and the aid of a camera; enables the surgeon to access the inside of the body without making large incisions

Leptin—a protein hormone made by adipocytes for regulating appetite and fat storage; helps maintain weight

Lymphocyte—a type of white blood cell in the immune system that fights infection and disease

Mast cells—immune cells that are present in connective tissue

Maturation phase—the final phase of wound healing that occurs after the wound has closed, also known as remodeling

Neurotransmitter—chemical messengers that the body can't function without

Neurodegenerative disorders—chronic conditions that damage and destroy parts of the nervous system over time, especially the brain

Neuroinflammatory signaling pathway—a complex biological response to inflammation that helps maintain homeostasis in the central nervous system

Neuroplasticity—the brain's ability to form, change, and reorganize synaptic connections

Neutrophil—a type of white blood cell in the immune system that fights infection and promotes wound healing

Nocturia—the need to regularly get up at night to urinate

Oxidative stress—disturbance in the balance between the production of free radicals and antioxidant defenses

Parasympathetic nervous system—a network of nerves that are part of the autonomic nervous system that relax the body after periods of stress

Pathogenesis—the manner by which a disease or disorder develops

Physiological—relating to the way a living organism functions

Physiology—the study of the functions and mechanisms of a living organism or system

Platelets—also known as thrombocytes, tiny, colorless blood cells that form clots and stop bleeding

Proliferative phase—the phase of wound healing focused on filling and covering the wound

Stressors—things that cause stress

Sympathetic nervous system—a network of nerves that helps the body activate the stress response

Triglycerides—the most common type of fat in your body, also known as lipids that circulate in your blood

Notes

3. SIGNS AND SYMPTOMS OF STRESS

[1] Brianna Chu, Komal Marwaha, Terrence Sanvictores, Ayoola O. Awosika, and Derek Ayers, "Physiology, Stress Reaction," *StatPearls [Internet]* (updated May 7, 2024), www.ncbi.nlm.nih.gov/books/NBK541120/.

[2] Ying Chen and John Lyga, "Brain-Skin Connection: Stress, Inflammation and Skin Aging," *Inflammation Allergy Drug Targets* 13(3) (June 2014): 177–90, https://doi.org/10.2174/1871528113666140522104422.

[3] P. S. MacLean, J. A. Higgins, E. D. Giles, V. D. Sherk, and M. R. Jackman, "The Role for Adipose Tissue in Weight Regain After Weight Loss," *Obesity Reviews* S 1 (January 22, 2015): 45-54, https://doi.org/10.1111/obr.12255.

[4] Salam Ranabir and K. Reetu, "Stress and Hormones," *Indian Journal of Endocrinology and Metabolism* 15, no. 1 (Jan–Mar 2011): 18-22, https://doi.org/10.4103/2230-8210.77573.

[5] Laren Thau, Jayashree Gandhi, and Sandeep Sharma, "Physiology, Cortisol," *StatPearls [Internet]* (updated August 29, 2022), www.ncbi.nlm.nih.gov/books/NBK538239/.

[6] Caroline P. Le and Erica K. Sloan, "Stress-Driven Lymphatic Dissemination: An Unanticipated Consequence of Communication Between the Sympathetic Nervous System and Lymphatic Vasculature," *Molecular & Cellular Oncology* 3, no. 4 (April 7, 2016), https://doi.org/10.1080/23723556.2016.1177674.

[7] Georgios Valsamakis, George Chrousos, and George Mastorakos, "Stress, Female Reproduction and Pregnancy," *Psychoneuroendocrinology* 100 (February 2019): 48-57, https://doi.org/10.1016/j.psyneuen.2018.09.031.

[8] Sulagna Dutta, Pallav Sengupta, Petr Slama, and Shubhadeep Roychoudhury, "Oxidative Stress, Testicular Inflammatory Pathways, and Male Reproduction," *International Journal of Molecular* 22, no. 18 (September 17, 2021): 10043, https://doi.org/10.3390/ijms221810043.

[9]Constantine Tsigos, Ioannis Kyrou, Eva Kassi, and George P. Chrousos, "Stress: Endocrine Physiology and Pathophysiology," *Endotext [Internet]* (updated October 17, 2020), www.ncbi.nlm.nih.gov/books/NBK278995/.

4. THE RELAXATION REMEDY

[1]Herbert Benson and William Proctor, *Relaxation Revolution* (New York: Scribner, 2010).

5. RESPOND HOLISTICALLY

[1]Syed Amin Tabish, "Complementary and Alternative Healthcare: Is it Evidence-based?," *International Journal of Health Sciences (Qassim)* 2, no. 1 (January 2008): v–ix, www.ncbi.nlm.nih.gov/pmc/articles/PMC3068720/.

6. RESUSCITATE YOUR POWER

[1]Tracie Braylock, "What I've Learned from My Accidental Home Birth," *Tracie Braylock* (blog), August 14, 2018, https://traciebraylock.com/what-ive-learned -from-my-accidental-home-birth/.

7. REVIEW YOUR SURROUNDINGS

[1]"Environmental Noise," in *Compendium of WHO and Other UN Guidance on Health and Environment, 2022 Update* (Geneva: World Health Organization, 2022), https://cdn.who.int/media/docs/default-source/who-compendium-on -health-and-environment/who_compendium_noise_01042022.pdf?sfvrsn=bc 371498_3.

[2]Evanthia Diamanti-Kandarakis, et al., "Endocrine-Disrupting Chemicals: An Endocrine Society Scientific Statement," *Endocrine Reviews* 30, no. 4 (June 2009): 293-342, https://doi.org/10.1210/er.2009-0002.

[3]Garth N. Graham, "Why Your ZIP Code Matters More Than Your Genetic Code: Promoting Healthy Outcomes from Mother to Child," *Breastfeeding Medicine* 11 no. 8 (October 2016): 396-97, https://doi.org/10.1089/bfm.2016.0113.

[4]Bonnie Sakallaris, et al., "Optimal Healing Environments," *Global Advances in Health and Medicine* 4, no. 3 (2015): 40-45, https://doi.org/10.7453/gahmj.2015.043.

[5]Chung-Heng Hsieh, et al., "The Effect of Water Sound Level in Virtual Reality: A Study of Restorative Benefits in Young Adults Through Immersive Natural Environments," *Journal of Environmental Psychology* 88 (June 2023), https://doi .org/10.1016/j.jenvp.2023.102012.

[6]Gaétan Chevalier, et al., "Earthing: Health Implications of Reconnecting the Human Body to the Earth's Surface Electrons," *Journal of Environmental and Public Health* (January 12, 2012), https://doi.org/10.1155/2012/291541.

[7]J. L. Oschman, G. Chevalier, and R. Brown, "The Effects of Grounding (Earthing) on Inflammation, the Immune Response, Wound Healing, and Prevention and Treatment of Chronic Inflammatory and Autoimmune Diseases," *Journal of Inflammation Research* 8 (March 24, 2015): 83-96, https://doi.org/10.2147/JIR.S69656.

8. RENEW YOUR MIND

[1]Christopher N. Cascio, et al., "Self-Affirmation Activates Brain Systems Associated with Self-Related Processing and Reward and Is Reinforced by Future Orientation," *Social Cognitive and Affective Neuroscience* 11, no. 4 (April 2016): 621-29, https://doi.org/10.1093/scan/nsv136.

9. REFUEL YOUR BODY

[1]Djésia Arnone, et al., "Sugars and Gastrointestinal Health," *Clinical Gastroenterology and Hepatology* 20, no. 9 (September 2022): 1912-24, https://doi.org/10.1016/j.cgh.2021.12.011.

[2]S. Noor, S. Piscopo, and A. Gasmi, "Nutrients Interaction with the Immune System," *Archives of Razi Institute* 76, no. 6 (December 30, 2021): 1579-88, https://doi.org/10.22092/ari.2021.356098.1775.

[3]Wang Lu, et al., "Antioxidant Activity and Healthy Benefits of Natural Pigments in Fruits: A Review," *International Journal of Molecular Scientists* 22, no. 9 (May 6, 2021): 4945, https://doi.org/10.3390/ijms22094945.

10. REST YOUR BODY

[1]David A. Kalmbach, Jason R. Anderson, and Christopher L. Drake, "The Impact of Stress on Sleep: Pathogenic Sleep Reactivity as a Vulnerability to Insomnia and Circadian Disorders," *Journal of Sleep Research* 27, no. 6 (May 24, 2018), https://doi.org/10.1111/jsr.12710.

[2]Christin Gerhardt, et al., "How Are Social Stressors at Work Related to Well-Being and Health? A Systematic Review and Meta-Analysis," *BMC Public Health* 21, no. 890 (2021), https://doi.org/10.1186/s12889-021-10894-7.

[3]M. Hirshkowitz, et al., "National Sleep Foundation's Updated Sleep Duration Recommendations: Final Report," *Sleep Health* 1, no. 4 (December 2015): 233-43, https://doi.org/10.1016/j.sleh.2015.10.004.

[4]Betty-Ann Heggie, "The Healing Power of Laughter," *Journal of Hospital Medicine* 14, no. 5 (May 2019): 320, https://doi.org/10.12788/jhm.3205.

11. RECONDITION YOUR BODY

[1]Tracie Braylock, "Receiving Rest," Proverbs 31 Ministries, April 24, 2020, https://proverbs31.org/read/devotions/full-post/2020/04/24/receiving-rest.

[2]Tracie Braylock, "Confidence is Key," Proverbs 31 Ministries, December 16, 2021, https://proverbs31.org/read/devotions/full-post/2021/12/16/confidence-is -key.

[3]Jung Ha Park, et al., "Sedentary Lifestyle: Overview of Updated Evidence of Potential Health Risks," *Korean Journal of Family Medicine* 41, no. 6 (November 2020): 365-73, https://doi.org/10.4082/kjfm.20.0165.

12. REALIGN YOUR SPIRIT

[1]Laura Upenieks, "Unpacking the Relationship Between Prayer and Anxiety: A Consideration of Prayer Types and Expectations in the United States," *Journal of Religion and Health* 62, no. 3 (June 2023): 1810-31, https://doi.org/10.1007/s10943 -022-01708-0.

13. REVIVE YOUR RELATIONSHIPS

[1]Susan K. Wood and Seema Bhatnagar, "Resilience to the Effects of Social Stress: Evidence from Clinical and Preclinical Studies on the Role of Coping Strategies," *Neurobiology of Stress* 1 (January 2015): 164-73, https://doi.org/10.1016/j.ynstr .2014.11.002.

About the Author

TRACIE BRAYLOCK is a holistic nurse educator, writer, and wellness consultant. As a former operating room nurse, she now advocates for mind-body-spirit well-being, holistic healing, and unapologetic relaxation. Her work has been featured in the American Holistic Nurses Association *Beginnings* magazine, Proverbs 31 Ministries, and Hallmark Mahogany, among others. Tracie teaches workshops, leads retreats, and lectures on issues related to nursing, writing, self-care, and healing lifestyles. She lives in northwest Ohio with her family.

Connect with Tracie:

https://traciebraylock.com

Facebook: @traciebraylock

Instagram: @traciebraylock

Social Media: @traciebraylock